T0328671

Cambridge Elements

Elements in New Religious Movements
Series Editor
Rebecca Moore
San Diego State University

Founding Editor
† James R. Lewis
Wuhan University

FIELDWORK IN NEW RELIGIOUS MOVEMENTS

George D. Chryssides
York St John University

CAMBRIDGE
UNIVERSITY PRESS

Shaftesbury Road, Cambridge CB2 8EA, United Kingdom

One Liberty Plaza, 20th Floor, New York, NY 10006, USA

477 Williamstown Road, Port Melbourne, VIC 3207, Australia

314–321, 3rd Floor, Plot 3, Splendor Forum, Jasola District Centre,
New Delhi – 110025, India

103 Penang Road, #05–06/07, Visioncrest Commercial, Singapore 238467

Cambridge University Press is part of Cambridge University Press & Assessment,
a department of the University of Cambridge.

We share the University's mission to contribute to society through the pursuit of
education, learning and research at the highest international levels of excellence.

www.cambridge.org
Information on this title: www.cambridge.org/9781009478694

DOI: 10.1017/9781009278713

First published 2024

A catalogue record for this publication is available from the British Library.

ISBN 978-1-009-47869-4 Hardback
ISBN 978-1-009-27873-7 Paperback
ISSN 2635-232X (online)
ISSN 2635-2311 (print)

Fieldwork in New Religious Movements

Elements in New Religious Movements

DOI: 10.1017/9781009278713
First published online: January 2024

George D. Chryssides
York St John University

Author for correspondence: George D. Chryssides,
gdchryssides@religion21.com

Abstract: New religious movements are often described as bizarre and sinister. Direct acquaintance, however, often gives a different impression from media portrayals and even from some academic writing – which is why fieldwork is important. After decades of undertaking fieldwork, George Chryssides discusses a number of his experiences, as well as studies by other scholars, and the issues that fieldwork involves. How do one's personal beliefs and lifestyle impinge on field research? How involved should a participant–observer become? How should we assess what we are told by insiders and by ex-members? What ethical problems does field research create? How should we engage in online fieldwork, arising from the increasing use of the Internet, accelerated by the Covid pandemic? These are among the issues which this Element explores, and which will be of interest both to field researchers, and to those who read about the fieldwork of others.

Keywords: cults, fieldwork, new religious movements, religion online, participant–observation, research ethics

ISBNs: 9781009478694 (HB), 9781009278737 (PB), 9781009278713 (OC)
ISSNs: 2635-232X (online), 2635-2311 (print)

Contents

Introduction

This short Element is not primarily a how-to manual. Its aim is not to provide advice on how to undertake fieldwork, but rather to discuss various salient issues that the practice of fieldwork poses. Students who need guidance on conducting fieldwork can safely be referred to Gregg and Scholefield's *Engaging with Living Religion: A Guide to Fieldwork in the Study of Religion* (2015) or the relevant parts of Chryssides and Geaves' *The Study of Religion* (2014).

Because of the concise nature of the volumes in this series, I have only given brief attention to questions about definitions of new religious movements (NRMs), typologies, and cult rhetoric. There are many discussions of these and other fundamental issues elsewhere. My slightly adapted version of Robert S. Ellwood and Harry B. Partin's definition, which allows an NRM to be up to 200 years old, enables me to comment on what are sometimes called the 'old new religions' and to draw on my own main specialist interest, Jehovah's Witnesses. In a few places I have strayed out of NRMs, using more traditional religions to illustrate points that are necessary in my discussion, to avoid creating hypothetical or fictitious scenarios.

Numerous examples in what follows are drawn from my own personal fieldwork, and I trust this is not self-indulgent. Since some of the ensuing discussion is about positionality, it may be helpful to declare where I am coming from. My background is in the Christian religion, and many years ago I was a student in training for a career in the Church of Scotland. After graduating in philosophy and systematic theology, I embarked on an academic career instead. When the Open University in the United Kingdom opened in 1973, I became a part-time tutor, and was assigned a role in their course entitled 'Man's Religious Quest' (later renamed 'The Religious Quest'). We were encouraged to take our students on field visits – something I had never done before, and we found it instructive to hear how adherents at the grassroots level understood their faiths, which was often different from the textbook versions.

My acquaintance with NRMs began in 1981, when I joined the Other Faiths Committee of the United Reformed Church, which had begun to define its stance on new religions. This brought me in contact with a number of NRMs, in the course of which I was invited to a Unification Church six-day seminar in Athens, an event which prompted me to write *The Advent of Sun Myung Moon* (1991). When I moved to the University of Wolverhampton in 1992, I inaugurated a new module on New Religious Movements, and was determined that the study of NRMs should be no different from that of traditional religions. Students were encouraged to listen at first hand to Unificationists, Hare Krishna devotees, Scientologists, and Jehovah's Witnesses, to visit their premises, and, where possible, to participate in their events. My prior training in biblical studies gave me some rapport with Jehovah's Witnesses, although our respective interpretations of scripture are miles apart, and it became evident that the literature about them was predominantly Christian evangelical polemic, with little scholarly discussion. My subsequent publications on the Watch Tower Bible and Tract Society were therefore an attempt to redress this imbalance. Because much of my own fieldwork is on Jehovah's Witnesses, readers may find a preponderance of examples taken from my research into the Watch Tower organisation, although I hope my experiences raise issues that go beyond a single NRM.

On one small point of detail, it should be noted that I have used the word 'informant', which I know is disliked by various colleagues, who prefer the term 'participant'. An informant is simply someone who provides information to the researcher, whereas participants are those who voluntarily and explicitly agree to be actively part of one's project. In fieldwork, our subjects do not necessarily agree explicitly to provide data, and in many cases what we write may be without our informants' knowledge. Obviously how we handle data and how we ensure our informants' privacy are matters which raise ethical issues, and which will be discussed in Section 5. In numerous instances I have not disclosed the name of the community being discussed: this is partly to protect their privacy, but also, since some organisations have a reputation for litigation, I would not wish to have to defend my comments outside the academic arena, even though I have taken the greatest precautions to ensure their veracity.

1 Foundations

One of my earliest introductions to fieldwork was a chance encounter with a young woman on a train. I was an early-career academic at the time, tutoring part-time for the Open University in the United Kingdom, where I had begun to teach its course on world religions, on which I then knew relatively little. The course material presented some fairly well-accredited schools of Mahayana Buddhism as eccentric fringe religious sects. Indeed, Trevor Ling's *History of Religions East and West*, which was a set text, describes Nichiren Buddhism as 'a gospel of struggle and aggression' (Ling 1967: 316), and states:

> The largest numerically and the best-known of these newly arisen sects is the Soka Gakkai. … The object of faith is a sacred formula Namu Myoho Rengekyo [*sic*] inscribed by the Buddhist leader Nichiren on a strip of paper. It is strongly nationalistic in character, it has also a strong millenarian quality and proclaims a coming millennium towards which men must direct

all their efforts. . . . The technique by which its converts are won is known as Shaku baku [*sic*], and consists of bombarding the potential convert with high-pressure propaganda until his resistance is overcome and he is 'converted'. (Ling 1967: 415)

Sitting opposite me on the train, the young woman was concentrating on a small red booklet bearing the title *Liturgy of the Nichiren Shoshu*. When she finally looked up, I asked her about it, and she told me more about the NRM that is now known as Soka Gakkai International (SGI). When we reached our destination, some of her friends alighted from an adjacent carriage, and I was introduced to them. They told me where they met, and I followed up our exchange by attending one of their *gongyo* meetings. In an attempt to establish a good rapport, I told them that I had read the Lotus Sutra, on which their teachings are based. 'Well, that's more than we have!' was the response, and I then discovered that the SGI members do not study the entire text, but chant two short chapters in Japanese, the Hoben and Juryo. They focus especially on the mantra *nam myoho renge kyo*, which is believed to contain the essence of the entire scripture, and to be exceedingly powerful in fulfilling one's desires and aspirations. I was told that their historical founder Nichiren (1222–1282) is regarded as a Buddha, unlike other Nichiren sects, who use a slightly different version of the mantra, and regard Nichiren as merely a bodhisattva. I was also surprised to be told that the goal of the Soka Gakkai was world peace, and that they understood *shakubuku* to mean encouragement rather than browbeating.

The story does not quite end there. I later discovered that some Buddhists had erected a pagoda in Battersea Park in London, which I decided to visit, and discovered that it belonged to the Nipponzan Myohoji, another Nichiren organisation. In conversation with one of the monks, I asked him why they regarded Nichiren as a bodhisattva rather than a Buddha. The question was met with some incredulity: he told me that, whether or not the SGI thought this was an important issue, it was of little interest to them, and not a key doctrine.

These two encounters reveal some important aspects of fieldwork. Although research involving fieldwork is frequently planned, often causing researchers to produce detailed outlines and timelines itemising the stages of the path of their research, it can sometimes be serendipitous and unpredicted. In my initial encounter, I was not in fact aware that I was undertaking fieldwork and would use the incident in subsequent writing; reciprocally, the SGI members did not know that they were informants, inadvertently being researched.

These incidents also point to the inappropriateness of defining religions by written texts, whether those of scholars, or their own sacred scriptures. For many centuries the study of religion has been text-based. Traditionally in the English-speaking world the available literature on Christianity has consisted of scriptures, Bible commentaries, theological treatises written by scholars, and histories of the Christian tradition, frequently hagiographical writings about saints and mystics. In the seminary in which I studied, the principal subjects were systematic theology, Old and New Testament, and ecclesiastical history. Considerable emphasis was given to the formation of the traditional Christian creeds, and the Christological controversies that led to their formulation. Most of the material that I studied has subsequently proved valuable, but its key aim was to ensure that students understood the difference between orthodoxy and heresy, and it resulted in scant attention being given to comparative religion, as it was then called, and nothing whatsoever on NRMs. Although aspiring ordinands were more likely to encounter Mormons (members of the Church of Jesus Christ of Latter-day Saints, or LDS) and Jehovah's Witnesses, than adherents to other traditional religions, their interpretations of the Bible were deemed unworthy of academic attention, being regarded as too idiosyncratic for serious discussion. By default, any knowledge we gained about NRMs was through extracurricular reading of Christian countercult material: Horton Davies' *Christian Deviations* (1954) and Walter Martin's *The Kingdom of the Cults* (1965) had recently been published, which evangelical Christians hailed as key works for understanding these organisations.

The limitations of Christian theology and the history of doctrine were not wholly obvious to us as students of religion. They focus on religious leaders rather than their followers, and they privilege the cognitive over the empirical. Most rank-and-file Christians simply do not know about theology and the history of doctrine, and are probably not unduly interested. When we learn of the early Christological disputes between Athanasius and Arius, which led to the formulation of the Nicene Creed, one cannot help wondering what the average fourth-century Christian made of them. Did they have arguments about whether or not Christ was 'eternally begotten of the Father' when they met in the marketplace, or did they simply not care, following whoever was leader of the congregation to which they belonged? When we read the accounts of saints and mystics, we are not learning of any religious experiences pertaining to the average Christian, and many of the accounts about them have little evidential backing.

The rejection of NRMs as being worthy of serious academic study in either biblical studies or in Christian theology caused the study of NRMs initially to be appropriated by sociologists, who found a place for it within the sociology of deviance. Early sociological treatment of NRMs took the form of developing theoretical models. Fieldwork came somewhat later, in part due to the lack of prominence and public interest before the second half of the twentieth century, and partly because foreign travel was expensive and difficult, which impeded both the influx of foreign religions and scholarly study abroad.

Pioneers of Fieldwork

Edward Burnett Tylor (1832–1917) is probably the best-known pioneer of anthropology. His best-known work, *Primitive Culture* (1871), was evolutionist in approach, contending that such study could shed light on the origins and developmental stages of 'modern' religion, and suggesting that civilisation progressed from 'savage' through 'barbarian' to 'civilised'. The term 'primitive' is, of course, pejorative, and subsequent scholars substituted the terms 'primal religion' and 'indigenous religion', although both these terms are also problematic (Harvey 2023b: 57–62). Bronislaw Malinowski (1884–1942), who spent two years between 1915 and 1917 in the Trobriand Islands of Papua New Guinea, has often been called 'the father of field research'. He rejected an evolutionary model, adopting a 'functionalist' approach to fieldwork: instead of merely noting the Islanders' practices, he held that they should be understood in terms of their function and purpose. Malinowski made a point of learning the language of the islanders, observing their customs and participating in their rituals. It was through his work that academia came to acknowledge the importance of social anthropology as a complement to textual studies. Subsequently E. E. Evans-Pritchard (1902–1973), who studied under Malinowski and ethnologist Charles Gabriel Seligman (1873–1940), undertook his work in Africa among the Azande and the Nuer. Evans-Pritchard defined the focus of his subject as 'primitive peoples'; nonetheless one important contribution to his study of the Azande was to contend that their beliefs in witchcraft magic and oracle consultation 'form a comprehensible system of thought . . . related to social activities, social structure, and the life of the individual' (Evans-Pritchard 1951: 4, 98), thus suggesting that there were other ways of looking at the world than those of westerners, by means of which they could organise their lives. Sociology of religion, in contrast with anthropology, has tended to focus on modern Western religious systems, although globalisation and internationalisation have blurred distinctions between 'our' culture and 'other' cultures. Many NRMs operate on an international level, and those who study them come from a variety of countries and ethnic backgrounds. Many NRM scholars prefer to be regarded as ethnologists, meaning that they focus on a specific group of people, with observation of human subjects being a key part of their activity.

Fieldwork is employed in a variety of subject areas, spanning biological sciences, archaeology, and a variety of aspects of human life including religion. It can be characterised as being conducted outside a laboratory or a library, studying its subject matter in its natural habitat, and can involve study of animals, the natural environment, and human subjects. In the case of fieldwork on NRMs, human subjects are of course the focus, and collection of data involves interviews, questionnaires, observation, participation, and most recently, studying materials made available online.

Although fieldwork is empirical, it is not experimental. Some time ago a group of psychologists set up an experiment to determine what proportion of Christian seminary students would put the parable of the Good Samaritan into practice and help someone in need (Darley and Batson 1973: 100–8). One of them acted the part of an injured person, whom the researchers' subjects would pass on their way to a predetermined destination. The experiment revealed that only a very small number of subjects would stop to offer help, indicating a large discrepancy between Christians' ideal conduct and their behaviour in practice. This is no doubt an interesting result, but it was a psychological experiment rather than an example of fieldwork, which does not seek to set up artificial scenarios, but observes religious behaviour, as far as possible, without changing the phenomenon. Having said this, however, there are occasions where I have tested out the boundaries of religious communities. In my early days of researching the Unification Church, it was rumoured that it was impossible to leave their premises. I investigated this popular accusation by seeing whether I would be permitted to walk as far as a telephone booth, where contact with outsiders would be possible. (It was not a problem, as I discovered.) There is a difference between setting up an experiment and testing boundaries, the latter sometimes being a necessary part of one's fieldwork.

Theoretical Issues

One cannot simply observe, however: appropriate observation requires prior knowledge and definite purpose. The philosopher of science Karl Popper once wrote:

> Twenty-five years ago I tried to bring home the same point to a group of physics students in Vienna by beginning a lecture with the following instructions: 'Take pencil and paper; carefully observe, and write down what you have observed!' They asked, of course, what I wanted them to observe. Clearly the instruction, 'Observe!' is absurd. (It is not even idiomatic, unless the object of the transitive verb can be taken as understood.) Observation is always selective. It needs a chosen object, a definite task, an interest, a point of view, a problem. And its description presupposes a descriptive language, with property words; it presupposes similarity and classification, which in their turn presuppose interests, points of view, and problems. (Popper 2002: 61)

Fieldwork requires a theoretical underpinning in order to make sense of the empirical data. First, there is the question of how NRMs are defined. The fact that public interest gained momentum in the 1960s and 1970s caused some scholars to define NRMs as phenomena that had arisen in the West in the postwar period (Clarke 1987: 5; Barker 1989: 9). As I have argued elsewhere (Chryssides 2012), such a definition is flawed on several grounds. First, NRMs are global phenomena and not exclusively Western. Second, the origins of many can be traced to a substantially earlier date. For example, Western Sufism can be traced back to 1910; the spiritual teacher George Gurdjieff (1866–1949) founded the Institute for the Harmonious Development of Man in France in 1922; Opus Dei, often regarded as an NRM, was founded in 1928; and Soka Gakkai was founded in Japan in 1930 (Chryssides 2012: 18–20). In addition, to focus on those NRMs that gained media attention in the 1960s and beyond is to bypass older religious communities that arose in an earlier period, but do not seem to feature so prominently in NRM studies. Examples include Swedenborgianism, Theosophy, Christadelphianism, Spiritualism, and Jehovah's Witnesses. While one can argue whether they should count as NRMs, there is no reason to suppose that they are less deserving of academic attention than Scientology, the Unification Movement, and The Family International.

There are other groups that are typically regarded as NRMs, but which maintain that they are ancient rather than new. Examples include Pagan organisations, which claim to revive ancient traditions; and the International Society for Krishna Consciousness (ISKCON), whose members follow what they believe to be the religion founded by Lord Krishna, whom they consider a historical figure who lived in Vrindaban around 3200 BCE. The famous mantra 'Hare Krishna' was taught by the Indian saint Chaitanya (c. 1485–1533). However, as organisations they are new, and, as Eileen Barker points out, they are characterised by having predominantly first-generation converts (Barker 1989: 11–12; Chryssides 2012: 19). For our present purposes, it should be noted that there exists a cluster of religious and spiritual organisations that are generally regarded by scholars as NRMs, and are typically the targets of the anticult and the Christian countercult movements.

Sociological Study

Of key importance in developing theoretical models is Max Weber (1864–1920), who distinguished between church and sect, the former being the dominant form of religion, which is responsible for key civic events, and to which members of society were deemed to belong by birth rather than conversion. The sect, by contrast, is a minority group which rejects some of the key beliefs or practices of the church (Weber 1956: 64–5). Weber's distinction was further developed by

Ernst Troeltsch (1865–1923), who added the category of mystical, to which he assigned groups that relied largely on personal religious experience. Sociologist Howard P. Becker (1899–1960) replaced Troeltsch's category of the mystical with the concept of cult. Essentially, the mystical or cult referred to those forms of spirituality that arose from outside the dominant religion or culture, for example organisations derived from Hindu or Buddhist traditions. Becker included Spiritualism, Theosophy, Christian Science, together with 'various pseudo-Hinduisms associated with Swamis and Yogis who consent, for a consideration, to carry their messages to the materialistic Western world' in his list (Becker 1932: 627–8).

These early attempts at defining typologies can now be seen to be inadequate. Using the term 'church' to refer to the dominant religion locks NRM studies into Western societies. Also, several of the terms mentioned earlier are pejorative, and would now be avoided by the majority of scholars, who would prefer the expression 'new religious movement' to the word 'cult' and would firmly reject terms like 'pseudo-Hinduism'. There have been subsequent attempts to improve categorisation. J. M. Yinger (1916–2011) suggested a distinction between acceptance sects, aggressive sects, and avoidance sects. The acceptance sect is a movement seeking internal reform, for example Opus Dei. The aggressive sect rejects society, for instance the Exclusive Brethren, while avoidance sects promote other-worldliness over worldly values, such as the Holiness Churches. Bryan Wilson (1926–2004) distinguished between conservationist sects, adventist/revolutionist sects, interventionist/pietist sects and gnostic sects, while Roy Wallis (1945–1990) proposed a threefold categorisation of NRMs into world-affirming, world-rejecting, and world-accommodating.

J. Gordon Melton and Robert L. Moore (1982) attempted a somewhat different approach, which categorised NRMs in terms of their religious pedigree. Their eightfold typology divided new religions into (1) Latter-day Saints; (2) communalists; (3) metaphysicians; (4) psychic-spiritualist movements; (5) Ancient Wisdom schools; (6) magical groups; (7) Eastern religions; and (8) Middle Eastern faiths (Melton and Moore 1982: 19–20). Arguably, new categories of NRMs have come to the fore since Melton and Moore defined this typology. For example, NRM scholars now recognise UFO-religions as a distinct category, and Paul Heelas has written substantially on what he labelled self-religions – organisations that emphasise human potential and self-improvement (see, e.g., Heelas 1988: 4–5). In the twenty-first century Carole Cusack (2010) has undertaken interesting work on what she calls invented religions – religions that have arisen out of fiction or parody, but have come to be taken seriously in certain circles as forms of religious expression (see Section 6).

Some of these sociological categories offer very blunt distinctions, at times making it difficult to pigeonhole specific organisations. For example, should we regard Jehovah's Witnesses as world-affirming or world-renouncing? They reject the values of the world's system of business, politics, and religion, yet they do not live apart from the world, and anticipate a final everlasting future in a transformed earthly paradise. It is not my purpose here to adjudicate among these competing typologies, but rather to comment on their relevance to field-work. In fact, pigeonholing is not always necessary, and how we categorise various NRMs depends on our purpose. What is important is that field researchers should be able to place the religious group being studied within a framework, and these various typologies suggest characteristics which might profitably be explored in empirical study. Of greater importance than to cat-egorise, say, the Unification Movement as world-rejecting or world-affirming, is for the fieldworker to examine how the organisation relates to the dominant culture and to traditional religions, how it regards conventional institutions such as marriage, what its attitude is to the world, and how its concept of the 'earth world' interacts with the 'spirit world'.

The Ideal and the Real

Since there are generally substantial differences between religion as it is portrayed, either in textbooks or by its religious hierarchies, and how religion is actually practised at the grassroots level, one prime function of fieldwork is to explore religion as it is followed by its practitioners. The distinction between written and practitioner versions is one that is difficult to characterise. The anthropologist Robert Redfield (1897–1958) attempted to distinguish between what he called the 'great tradition' and the 'little tradition'. Redfield studied the Mexican Tepoztlán people, who were a small agrarian community, which made his study manageable. Being removed from city life, they constituted the little tradition, which contrasted with the allegedly more definitive versions that are characteristic of the taught versions of their beliefs and practices. Redfield wrote:

> The great tradition is cultivated in schools and temples; the little tradition works itself out and keeps itself going in the lives of the unlettered in their village communities. (Redfield 1956: 70)

Redfield's distinction is no longer widely accepted. The terminology of great and little reduces the importance and legitimacy of those who practise versions of the religion that diverge from the taught versions. It could also be questioned whether those living in rural communities are less educated and less able to understand the taught versions of the religion and culture.

Other attempts to identify different levels of religion involve distinguishing between official and popular versions of religion (Vrijhof and Waardenburg 1977). For example, Christianity's official teaching, as expressed in the Nicene Creed, is that Jesus Christ is 'eternally begotten of the Father', yet, according to a recent survey some 75 per cent of Protestant evangelicals agreed to the statement, 'Jesus is the first and greatest being created by God' (Weber 2018). No doubt these respondents were familiar with the famous Christmas hymn 'O come, all ye faithful', which contains the words 'Very God, begotten not created', referring of course to Jesus Christ. The distinction between official and popular is not a clear one: traditional hymns tend to be written by Christians who are highly educated,[1] yet they are sung by people throughout society, even though those who sing may fail to understand the full import of the words. Congregational singing is a somewhat neglected aspect of fieldwork, but it serves as a crossroads between theology and popular practice.

Another attempt to distinguish between different layers of religion might be to contrast the ideal and the real. The 'ideal' Christian ought to understand and believe the traditional creeds, and observe fundamental Christian practices like keeping the Ten Commandments and loving one's neighbour. Yet, as the Good Samaritan experiment demonstrated, most Christians fall short of their religion's standards. Unfortunately, textbook versions of religions tend to focus on religious hierarchies and spiritual virtuosos, such as Saint Francis of Assisi and Mother Teresa, who were not at all typical of the average Christian. One contribution of fieldwork, therefore, can be to identify the rank-and-file practice of a religion which underlies these ideal versions.

A further endeavour to define popular practice involves the term 'folk religion', which has gained popularity. The term's origins can be traced back to 1901, when Paul Drews (1858–1912), a German Lutheran pastor, used it to alert his ordinands to local variations to the church liturgy that they were likely to encounter. The term subsequently found its way into folklore studies, but without agreed meaning. The preferred term among folklorists now tends to be 'vernacular religion', meaning, as Leonard Primiano puts it, 'religion as it is lived: as human beings encounter, understand, interpret, and practice it' (Primiano 1995: 44).

Religious Writings

Although fieldwork in NRMs predominantly involves studying human subjects, the scholar cannot afford to neglect their religious writings. It is important to distinguish various types of written material, and note how practitioners regard

---

[1] Frederick Oakeley (1802–1880), who wrote the carol, was a clergyman and prebendary at Lichfield Cathedral.

them. Some NRMs accept already existing writings belonging to their parent tradition: for example, Messianic Jews accept the Torah; New Christian groups such as the Exclusive Brethren and The Family International accept the veracity of the Bible; groups derived from Islam will regard the Qur'an as a definitive text. In addition, many NRMs have their own publications, which fall into a variety of categories. Some are given canonical status, for example The Book of Mormon for members of the LDS Church. The Church of Scientology has defined the totality of L. Ron Hubbard's non-fictional writings as scripture. Other publications may be liturgical manuals or organisational rule books, and these can tell us much about a community's treatment of its worship, rites of passage, and disciplinary procedures. If the researcher wants to know how the Unification Church deals with birth, marriage, and death, its liturgical manual *The Tradition* tells us much more than is possible through regular fieldwork. At times, the status of a publication can be ambiguous. For example, it is unclear whether the Unification Church's *Exposition of Divine Principle* is a new scripture, or whether it is a theological treatise. Jehovah's Witnesses have a slightly complex position regarding sacred texts – the Bible is the infallible bedrock of their faith, but is interpreted through the Watch Tower Society's publications. Their publications serve different functions: some prescribe the format to be observed at congregation meetings, while *The Watchtower* offers the Society's interpretation of scripture, which does not claim infallibility, but from which publicly expressed dissent is unacceptable. *Awake!* magazine focuses more on items of general human interest, although in recent times the organisation has expressed the view that it should give more attention to spiritual matters. Although frequently accused of shifting its doctrinal position, the Society openly publishes 'adjustments in view' when changes of interpretation have occurred. The role of fieldwork is instrumental in identifying the status that is given to publications, and often it is informants who can highlight articles which are regarded as important, and when key changes occur.

Unlike traditional religions, whose scriptures have been written in the distant past, and with which their followers are often unfamiliar, an NRM's own publications are more likely to be definitive in understanding their faith, and tend to be studied and known by their followers. There is also less likelihood of divergences between the beliefs and practices, as defined by the leaders, and what happens at grassroots level. This is because, as Eileen Barker observes, at least in the early stages of an NRM's existence, those who belong are first-generation converts (Barker 1989: 11–12). They do not belong to their faith by default, as is characteristic of many sectors of the dominant religion, but have joined their chosen NRM after being instructed in its teachings and practices, and have made the active decision to follow them. When the anticult movement suggests that they are subjected to intensive indoctrination (brainwashing or mind control, as they often call the process of instruction), they are drawing attention to the fact that teachings that were initially unfamiliar when outside the organisation have had to be imparted, understood, learned, and reinforced through continued teaching. Jehovah's Witnesses are continually instructed in the religion through their twice-weekly meetings, in which the Bible is explained (according to their own interpretation), through their publications *The Watchtower* and *Awake!* magazines, and increasingly through the voluminous amount of material that is found on their website JW.org. It would be impossible to undergo baptism to become a Jehovah's Witness without having to satisfy its congregational elders that one had a thorough understanding of their teachings, and led a lifestyle that was commensurate with the organisation's expectations. Fieldwork cannot be done in a vacuum, but must be undertaken in the light of the organisation's published writings.

It is worth noting that, where an NRM draws on ancient religious texts such as the Bible, the fieldworker is not so concerned with the original meaning, but rather with the reception by the community being studied. In the field of traditional biblical studies, scholars prefer to discuss what the original authors meant, for example, how the various Greek words that are translated as 'love' should be understood. By contrast, the Children of God (now The Family International) were noted for offering sexual favours to seekers, in the name of love, and one of founder–leader David Berg's MO Letters asserts, with complete disregard for biblical scholarship, that 'the carnal love is a part of the spiritual love' (Berg 1977). The authors' original meaning is left behind, superseded by the understanding of the new religious community, raising the issue of ownership of the interpretation of scripture. The postmodern thinker Roland Barthes is renowned for his expression 'the death of the author', suggesting new rules for interpreting a text, and whether the understanding of traditional religious texts is left behind by various new religious movements. NRM studies regards these understandings as interesting and important in their own right.

Conclusion

This section has identified several reasons for undertaking fieldwork. Being new, many NRMs are insufficiently documented, or receive unfair or inadequate coverage by the media and by their critics; hence scholars have an obligation to correct misunderstandings, and to ensure the dissemination of fair and reliable information. We are presenting NRMs as they are practised, rather than relying on accounts that idealise, denigrate, or stereotype. The methods of the fieldworker involve direct contact with adherents, using observation, participant–observation, interviewing, and sometimes questionnaire work. Although research is normally planned in advance, particular value should nonetheless be attached to incidental fieldwork, in which adherents volunteer information, which reflects what they want to tell the researcher, rather than what the researcher has decided to elicit. (My term 'incidental fieldwork' is prompted by the Jehovah's Witnesses' expression 'incidental witnessing' to designate unscheduled opportunities to spread their message when not undertaking house-to-house evangelising or staffing literature carts.) Although fieldwork is not predominantly library-based, there exists a symbiotic relationship between the practice of religion and published literature, in particular the texts that followers use, and how they are understood. It should also be remembered that NRMs never stand alone in isolation from the rest of society, and from their religious antecedents. It is therefore important to see how they relate to the dominant culture, to mainstream religion, and to each other.

2 Landmark Studies

In order to understand NRMs that derive from traditional religions, some knowledge of their pedigree is necessary. By the nineteenth century, Western scholarship was beginning to widen its focus from the Christian tradition in which it was situated. Towards the end of the nineteenth century, with the inception of "comparative religion" (as it was then called), much work was done by scholars such as Max Müller, Monier Monier-Williams, and Rhys Davids in acquiring, principally, Hindu and Buddhist texts and translating them. Their existence gave rise to linguistic studies but, important though these texts are, they had relatively little place in the lives of the average Hindu and Buddhist.

This work was anticipated, however, by a limited number of empirical studies in the eighteenth century, as a consequence of the European colonisation of Africa and Asia, and the rise of Christian missionary activity. William Jones (1746–1794) served in Calcutta, where he studied the Indian law code, the *Dharma Shastras*, and wrote a treatise *On the Gods of Greece, Italy and India*. The missionary William Ward (1769–1823) wrote a four-volume work entitled *Account of the Writings, Religion and Manners of the Hindoos* (1818). Neither of these works involved fieldwork, as we know it today, but were based to a considerable extent on what the authors had observed of Indian culture. By today's standards of scholarship neither study could be considered satisfactory. Jones adopted an evolutionary approach to religion, while Ward's missionary stance resulted in a highly derogatory account of Indian spirituality, highlighting practices such as *sati* (the immolation of Indian widows), child marriage, infanticide, and the erotic aspects of the *Puranas*, which he described as 'filth', commenting that 'their very temples are polluted with filthy images, and their acts of worship tend to inflame the mind with licentious ideas' (Ward 1817: xxix).

Also worthy of mention is Laurence Waddell (1854–1938), who undertook some pioneering work on Buddhism in Tibet. Waddell was an army medical officer who was stationed in India, Burma, and Tibet. Having learned Sanskrit and Tibetan, he studied Tibetan religious practices when he was in Darjeeling, and became the cultural consultant on Francis Younghusband's invasion of Tibet in 1903–1904. He is most famed for his *The Buddhism of Tibet* (1895), involving fieldwork which went to the extent of purchasing a Tibetan monastery, and asking its monks to demonstrate the various rituals that they performed in it – something that few fieldworkers today would be able to do! Waddell's account of Buddhism has been much criticised: it is colonialist, describing the Tibetans as 'primitive people' (1895: 450). It uses terminology that would now be considered inappropriate, for example terms like 'demonolatry' and 'Buddhist eucharist'. Nonetheless, when one takes into consideration the paucity of knowledge about Tibetan religion and culture at the time, Waddell's account was a remarkable achievement. If Waddell is at times disparaging, this should be contrasted with the idealised perception of Tibet before the 1959 Chinese invasion which is typically found within Western expressions of Buddhism, with the exception of the New Kadampa Tradition. New forms of Buddhism cannot be understood without wider knowledge of Buddhism, and the organisation's understanding of its history, practices, and tensions among Buddhist groups.

Until the late twentieth century, much of the writing on NRMs was evaluative and often pejorative, although more restrained than Ward; it was largely penned by evangelical Protestant Christian apologists. It is not altogether clear whether these authors derived their information from direct contact with exponents of these organisations. They appear to be mainly concerned with their doctrines, rather than their practices and lifestyle, and hence endeavoured to compare groups' written material with the teachings of mainstream Christianity. In many cases these writings demonstrate little knowledge of the organisations under discussion, but focus more on the Christian teachings that they believe should replace them. One remarkable exception is a compilation by C. Maurice Davies, entitled *Unorthodox London*, published in 1873. Davies was an Anglican clergyman who made a point of attending meetings of minority religious organisations, including Christadelphians, Unitarians, Tabernacle Ranters, Plymouth Brethren, Spiritualists, and Swedenborgians. These brief accounts were originally published in the *Daily Telegraph*, and their tone is decidedly empathetic, as is indicated by the cover page which bears the text 'In my Father's house are many mansions' (John 14:2). These are brief journalistic snapshots, which of course fall considerably short of what we would count as fieldwork today, but they have the merit of being first-hand empirical observations of religious communities on which little had been written.

Some Landmark NRM Studies

More recently, a number of studies stand out as important published writings involving fieldwork. One early, and much-cited, piece of research is *When Prophecy Fails* (1956) by Leon Festinger, Henry W. Riecken, and Stanley Schachter. Festinger and his collaborators infiltrated a small group they called Sananda, whose leader 'Mrs Keech' – now known to be Dorothy Martin – claimed to receive messages by means of automatic writing, predicting a great flood which would affect everyone from the Arctic Circle to the Gulf of Mexico. Those who heeded this warning could escape the catastrophe by being escorted to a place of safety. There they would await the arrival of extraterrestrials, who would take them to the planet Clarion, or some other planet, where they would be instructed and purified to return to a renewed earth, which they could then repopulate with upright people (Festinger et al. 1956: 62).

The object of Festinger's research was to determine how a group would deal with cognitive dissonance – that is, the discrepancy between declared belief and proven facts – and what effect the failure of expectations might have on group coherence. When neither the predicted deluge nor the arrival of extraterrestrials occurred, the group at first explained away their non-appearance, revising their expectations. The researchers concluded that an individual's beliefs were resistant to change when they were held with deep conviction and the believer had invested considerable time and energy, making reappraisal difficult. Disconfirmation occurred where the belief was specific and hence manifestly falsified by the evidence. In such a situation, belonging to a community of believers offered support, facilitating faith maintenance. Hence, as it became clear that Mrs Keech's predictions had failed, loyalty nevertheless prevailed over reason, and the group's fervour increased, rather than diminished.

Festinger's study was conducted over an extensive period of time, and was therefore considerably expensive but, although highly influential, it has been criticised on a number of grounds. The number of researchers involved amounted at times to nearly one third of the Sananda group, and thus influencing their choices, and causing the project to suffer from data contamination. The covertness of the research has also attracted criticism on ethical grounds. In all probability such an investigation would be stopped in its tracks today by a university ethics committee. A less frequent, but nonetheless important, criticism is the researchers' understanding of prophecy, which they regarded simply as prediction, and particularly failed prediction. It is unfortunate that subsequent scholars have shared this faulty assumption, against which I have argued elsewhere (Chryssides 2010: 27–48).

A second landmark publication is John Lofland's *Doomsday Cult: A Study of Conversion, Proselytization, and Maintenance of Faith* (1966), which is the earliest participant–observer study of the Unification Church. Lofland, however, adopted the pseudonym of 'The Divine Precepts' for the organisation, concealing its identity, which was not widely known in the period 1959–1963, when the researchers studied them. Its leader is given the pseudonym Mr. Chang, and the missionary in 'Bay City' is a Miss Yoon Sook Lee, who was in reality the Unification Church's late Korean scholar, Young Oon Kim. Lofland's aim was to ascertain how countercultural groups recruit, how people become involved in them, and how they maintain such involvement. Lofland recounts how Miss Lee managed to assemble a small study group of a dozen seekers, and attempted to interest the public through leafleting, advertising, and press releases, followed by personal letters to individuals. She also made presentations at religious gatherings, not disclosing her connections. Inviting seekers into the group's own physical premises proved marginally more productive, although enquirers were reluctant to listen to recorded lectures that lasted four and a half hours. Lofland identifies various types of enquirer: the repeatedly disorganised, freeloaders who sought non-religious benefits, inveterate serial seekers, those embarking on a spiritual quest, and counter-missionaries who sought to dissuade members from remaining.

A third piece of research is worth mentioning, namely that of Robert Balch and David Taylor on the organisation that became known as Heaven's Gate, and whose members collectively committed suicide in 1997. This research is particularly interesting since it was conducted in 1975, more than twenty years before the suicides, at a time when the group was unknown to the general public. In a number of articles in psychology journals, the researchers describe attending lectures by Marshall Herff Applewhite and Bonnie Lu Nettles, whom they observed by joining an early group of followers. The articles depict their lifestyle of camping and seeking support from outsiders. They describe how Bo and Peep (as the leaders called themselves at the time) went into seclusion after dividing the group into cells of typically fourteen members. After their fieldwork, the researchers contacted ex-members by means of snowball sampling and interviewed thirty-one of them. Balch and Taylor report that Bo and Peep's presentations were not aggressively proselytising, but rather attracted those who had previous interest in flying saucers and psychic phenomena, and were seeking personal growth (Balch and Taylor 1977).

The previous three examples of early NRM research were all covert studies, raising important ethical issues, which will be discussed in a later section. The fact that Festinger and Lofland used pseudonyms for the groups they studied underlines the fact that academic interest at the time lay in the sociology of deviance rather than the religious systems in their own right. Over half a century later, it would be unthinkable that any scholar would write about the Unification Church without mentioning its identity.

A fourth highly influential piece of research was done overtly by Eileen Barker, whose *The Making of a Moonie: Choice or Brainwashing?* (1984) is a landmark study. Faced with the popular belief that those who join NRMs are brainwashed by a charismatic leader, Barker's key research question was how well-educated young people could come to accept a seemingly strange and unnatural lifestyle and set of beliefs, which were radically different from those of their parents and friends. The notion of brainwashing, of course, lacks clear definition, and is not widely accepted among NRM scholars, but only by the media, the anticult movement, a handful of unsympathetic academics, and the general public (Introvigne 2022a). Her study, conducted in the late 1970s and early 1980s, involved in-depth interviews, questionnaires, and two years of participant–observation, which involved attending Unification Church workshops and living in UC communities, including Camp K (Maacama Hill) and Boonville (both in California), which had become notorious as highly guarded indoctrination centres from which escape was impossible. Barker's findings were that, of the 1,017 workshop attendees in the London area in 1979, only 15 per cent completed the 21-day workshop; 10 per cent accepted full-time or part-time membership for over a week; and a mere 4 per cent were still affiliated by January 1983; only 3.5 per cent of the original 1,017 remained full-time members at the beginning of that year. Of those who made an initial visit to a Unification centre, a minuscule 0.005 per cent had any association with the UC after two years. These statistics suggest that, far from practising irresistible brainwashing, recruitment of new members was extremely difficult, and the vast majority of seekers voluntarily decided against joining the organisation. If a university had such a poor progression rate, it would soon be closed down!

The Function of Fieldwork

Eileen Barker's work has been particularly influential in providing a focus for NRM Studies and for bringing together scholars and other stakeholders in the subject. Before *The Making of a Moonie*, the NRM publications market was saturated mainly with Christian evangelical literature. A small number of scholarly monographs existed, which tended to provide general overviews of a variety of NRMs rather than focused studies of individual organisations, and it was unclear to what extent the authors based their information on personal fieldwork. The establishment of INFORM (Information Network Focus on Religious Movements) in 1988 at the London School of Economics provided a forum for scholars, members of the public, and – importantly – members of new religions themselves to come together and listen first-hand to each other. In the same year, in Torino, Italy, CESNUR (Center for Studies on New Religions) was founded, also bringing together scholars and members of NRMs. At CESNUR's international conferences it is common practice to include a field visit, enabling participants to further their direct acquaintance with religious exponents.

It may be asked what point there is in researching NRMs, which are typically small spiritual communities. When I was attempting to publish my first book on NRMs, *The Advent of Sun Myung Moon* (1991), one of the reviewers of my proposal commented that he did not see the value of studying a small minority group that positioned itself outside mainstream religion. This was a somewhat surprising comment. Although the Unification Church in the United Kingdom only had around 500 members, its worldwide affiliation was much greater, with reportedly some 3,000,000 members at the time (Adherents.com 2019). Many new religions are actually quite large, with adherents to individual organisations often exceeding that of the world's traditional faiths. Some groups are small, of course, although the influence and the publicity they receive may well justify the attention they are given.

There can be various reasons for researching small groups. They can be regarded as microcosms – communities that are manageable in size for the researcher, and which can shed light on how larger organisations function. They can also grow larger with the passage of time, and our ability to discover their origins and their early stages of development can be instructive. John Lofland's *Doomsday Cult* gives an important insight into the early years of an organisation, how its missionary activity developed, and how it achieved the impact that it subsequently made. Also, one never knows when a little-known group will become noteworthy. The Heaven's Gate group was unfamiliar to the public, and almost entirely unknown even to NRM scholars when the news of the suicides broke in 1997. If it had not been for Robert Balch and David Taylor's fieldwork, we would have lacked any scholarly background on the incident.

A further, and more obvious, function of publishing our work is to disseminate accurate information, which the public generally gain through media reports. The media are not renowned for their accuracy or impartiality, and because their objectives seem to be commercial, they tend to focus on stories that sell rather than more balanced and potentially less exciting material.

Readers appear to have a greater appetite for stories about sexual abuse in NRMs, rather than any good work that some of them may do, or whether, for example, the incidence of sexual abuse is greater or less than in other religious or secular organisations. Television discussions are often designed to provoke controversy rather than to elicit objective information. In one television discussion to which I was invited, the producers seated an Orthodox rabbi next to a representative of Jews for Jesus – hardly a recipe for friendly debate. In this programme, the theme was 'What's the difference between a cult and a religion?', which was undoubtedly a question designed to reinforce misconceptions and to foster muddled thinking, but was nonetheless taken up with alacrity. Out of about a dozen participants, only one was an academic who specialised in ancient Hebrew history, rather than new religions. Inevitably, one prominent member of the anticult movement participated, identified as a cult expert. So-called cult experts are largely unqualified to speak about NRMs, and cannot possibly have expertise on the enormous number of new religions that have come into being worldwide. Nonetheless, these are the people who are often given credence by the media, gaining public attention by highlighting the violence and abuse that are attributed to NRMs.

Fieldworkers study NRMs at first-hand, in order to examine directly what their members believe and practice, rather than through second-hand accounts. Fieldwork generally explores a single religion, or even a single community. Unlike the cult expert, they do not claim expertise on NRMs generally, and many scholars have gained recognition for work on one specific NRM, or have even specialised more specifically on a particular topic within it, such as its history in a particular country, the status of women, or the practice of child-rearing.

A related function of fieldwork is to fill in the gaps in our knowledge of contemporary religion. Because of the newness of NRMs, many have eluded serious academic treatment, particularly in their infancy. Even after decades of scholarly attention, some still remain undocumented, and many only partially recorded. Despite the large amount of popular material on Jehovah's Witnesses, until recently there has been little serious academic writing on them. The appropriation of NRM studies by sociologists has resulted in research into themes such as the effectiveness of their evangelising, or occupational and social class. Such studies are not unimportant, but they leave unexamined themes that one would normally take on board in the study of traditional religions, such as their sources of authority, and how they treat rites of passage, such as birth, marriage, and death. These are gaps I have endeavoured to fill by my own fieldwork on the Watch Tower organisation (Chryssides 2016, 2022).

Because new religions are new, they are in the process of evolving, and an important function of fieldwork is to monitor change. Popular perception often defines NRMs in terms of their founder–leaders. While writing this Element, I was approached by a journalist who sought my views on how people can become 'vulnerable to the gurus'. Few people can imagine the Unification Church without thinking of Sun Myung Moon, Scientology without L. Ron Hubbard, or The Family International without David Berg and his somewhat outrageous MO Letters. Yet David Berg, Swami Prabhupada, Herbert Armstrong, L. Ron Hubbard, Elizabeth Clare Prophet, Maharishi Mahesh Yogi, Rajneesh/Osho, and Sun Myung Moon, have all died, and can no longer be personally influential in their followers' conversion narratives or spiritual instruction. Indeed, even during their lifetimes, their organisations had grown too large for direct contact with the leader to be a typical occurrence. Instead, the founder's death raises other important issues: charismatic leadership, the problem of succession, and whether and how the organisation will maintain its institutional structures in the absence of these founder–leaders. People who were young novice members of communities when I initially started my research on NRMs are now the elder statesmen and stateswomen, often in positions of high authority. Issues of charisma, succession, ageing, and generally changing, are therefore all matters which cannot find their way into the literature without field research.

It is not merely leaders who die, but members themselves. Initially members of NRMs were concerned with absorbing the teachings of the founder–leader, learning the practices, spreading the message, fundraising, and often living in communities. As the NRM has matured, issues arise relating to marriage, child-rearing, and finally dying. These stages of life raise their own questions, which are often not anticipated in the organisation's inception, and therefore go undocumented. The field researcher thus has the task of noting how children are raised within the movement – how they are disciplined, how they learn the beliefs and practices, and how their level of commitment is affected by being second-generation, rather than first. Issues about community life also need reappraisal in some cases. One of my informants in the Unification Church told me he was finding difficulty in living as a family in a single room in the organisation's headquarters. It was originally assigned when he and his wife were a single couple, but the organisation would not provide larger facilities when they started a family. The problem is often resolved by members making the transition from living in community to finding their own home, with the result that different types of membership – for example community and home – can emerge. Fieldwork can thus enable diachronic study of NRMs as well as synchronic.

NRM Critics

Public perception of NRMs tends to be negative. Heaven's Gate is one of several NRM disasters that have caused the public to be wary of NRMs. Many recall Jonestown, Waco, the Solar Temple, and Aum Shinrikyo, which have caused apprehensiveness about involvement with NRMs, and some opponents have even cautioned against field research. Ian Haworth, of the Cult Information Centre (United Kingdom), writes:

> Accurate information on cults is not best obtained by trying to infiltrate a cult. This is far too dangerous. (Haworth 2001: 8)

The danger that most concerns NRM critics is brainwashing, creating fear that they might be subjected to an involuntary process of indoctrination, which makes joining the organisation irresistible.

Certainly, some NRMs can put pressure on researchers, believing that, in common with the seekers, they are potential converts. During my last week of fieldwork on the Unification Church, which involved a seven-day residential seminar, I was repeatedly questioned on what I thought of the previous lecture, and whether I was persuaded by it; it was barely possible to have a meal without such interrogation. I later learned that the British Unification president had specifically instructed my 'spiritual parent', who had accompanied me, to do this. However, I have never found resistance difficult, and I do not know of any scholars who have been converted to the NRM they have studied. There is a potential risk of physical danger, however, if one is researching a far-right group, and there have been instances where an NRM has threatened to sue a researcher for alleged defamation. Calling an NRM a cult, which is something that the anticult movement frequently does, invites risk of litigation. Health and safety issues should also be a fairly obvious concern: on at least two occasions I have suffered as a result of poor hygiene conditions in food preparation. There are risks in studying NRMs, but probably not the ones that critics allege. The same is true of traditional religions, where I have had similar experiences regarding food.

A further criticism of fieldwork among NRMs is that researchers risk becoming what are known as cult apologists. Opponents of new religions frequently allege that NRMs will only show us their favourable aspects, about which they hope we will write, providing unduly positive assessments. NRM scholars are accused of talking to members – those who remain insiders and positive about their experiences – and not to ex-members, distressed families, or victims of cult abuse. It is certainly true that there have been researchers who have given unduly positive assessments of NRMs. It is unfortunate, for example, that some researchers have claimed that Scientology auditing (their form of counselling) is a form of worship (Kliever 1994), and that founder–leader L. Ron Hubbard was significantly influenced by major world religions like Hinduism and Buddhism (Berglie 1996). Even experienced scholars can make mistakes, as happened when J. Gordon Melton and James R. Lewis visited the Aum Shinrikyo headquarters after the 1995 sarin gas attacks on the Tokyo underground, and were persuaded at the time that Aum was not responsible (Lewis 2019). Academics are not infallible, although their fallibility presents a case for vigilance and critical assessment of the data that they find. It is also not true that NRM scholars are unfamiliar with family problems, vulnerability, and ex-member testimony. Again, parents, those feeling victimised, and ex-members also must be treated with caution, since they may not necessarily be typical, and they too have their biases. How we maintain a middle path between being critics and being apologists is a difficult tightrope to walk. The extent to which the NRM fieldworker can take sides in a controversy is likely to be is an issue about which NRM researchers continue to be vigilant.

3 Positionality

Most anthropologists are familiar with the maxim 'making the strange familiar and the familiar strange'. The expression is sometimes attributed to the German philosopher Georg Philipp Friedrich von Hardenberg (aka Novalis, 1772–1801), but its origins are uncertain. Those who study new religious movements often find themselves entering strange worlds. Why would anyone be persuaded to give up a well-paid job, as some did, to follow Marshall Herff Applewhite and Bonnie Lu Nettles, believing them to be the two prophets mentioned in the Book of Revelation, and lead a nomadic spartan lifestyle, culminating in mass suicide? Why should anyone believe that Sun Myung Moon is the messiah, when there are many messianic claimants? Moreover, to those outside the Unification Church he appears totally lacking in the charisma his followers find in him. The media and the anticult movement typically describe such movements with adjectives like 'bizarre', 'wacky', and 'absurd', but, more often than not, as Evans-Pritchard noted when studying the Azande, on closer acquaintance they can be found to display an internal and fairly coherent logic, even if the outsider does not find it compelling. Fieldwork is an important way of reducing the distance between the world of the NRM member and more conventional reality, and the task of the scholar is to present these beliefs and practices in a clear, empathetic, and systematic way.

Phenomenological Approaches

In the nineteenth and twentieth centuries phenomenologists of religion wrote about a 'bridge of understanding'. They included Nathan Söderblum (1866–1931), Rudolf Otto (1869–1937), Gerardus van der Leeuw (1890–1950), Joachim Wach (1889–1955), and Mircea Eliade (1907–1986). Their basic quest was to find the 'essence' of religion. Christians might have their own various concepts of God, for example, but these no doubt differ from the Jew, the Muslim, and the Zoroastrian. They certainly differ from that of the Krishna devotee, and of course Buddhist groups do not acknowledge a creator God, although they believe in the existence of a variety of supernatural beings. The difference cannot lie in the external reality, since it is believed to exist independently of our perceptions, so the phenomenologists' recommendation was to practise *epoché* – bracketing one's assumptions – and traversing this bridge of understanding in order to achieve what they called 'eidetic vision', which meant seeing the true form (Greek, *eidos*) as it really is. This ultimate reality, of course, cannot be called God, since that concept belongs to the Abrahamic faiths, so instead Otto identified this essence as 'the holy' and 'the numinous', while Eliade wrote about 'the sacred'. Although these categories are problematic, they are of some use in the study of NRMs, since one can distinguish between ones that are firmly empirical, and those, such as the Church of Scientology, whose members seldom talk about God, but appear to have more pragmatic concerns.

The philosopher and scholar of religion Ninian Smart (1927–2001) is sometimes said to be the last of the phenomenologists, although he preferred the term 'structured empathy'. While attaching some merit to Otto's concept of the numinous, Smart was instrumental in widening the study of religion beyond Christianity. By 'structured empathy' he means endeavouring to enter the believer's thought world without either endorsing it or rejecting it, and analysing and classifying the data (Smart 1979: 8–9). Smart cites the saying, 'we should not judge a person until we have walked a mile in his or her moccasins' (Smart 1995: 6). The reference to moccasins is to alert the reader to the difference in lifestyle of the community under study, a phenomenon that becomes increasing apparent in the study of new religions. (Smart attributes the proverb to Native Americans, but it actually comes from the nineteenth-century American poet Mary T. Lathrap.)

Most scholars now recognise the problems with the 'bridge of understanding' model. The notion that scholars can somehow bracket their assumptions and shake off their prejudices is, of course, impossible. It is not possible to identify all of one's prejudices, which remain largely concealed, even from the researcher, until they are pointed out or come to light through acquaintance with a different worldview, although some assumptions and prejudices can at least be reduced. The fact that I am the researcher immediately creates a bias: the very fact that I select the NRMs that I study is itself a predilection. My own choice of studying predominantly Christian-derived organisations tells readers something about me, and not simply the movements themselves, and other scholars will make different choices, depending on their predilections. I can only have direct experience of the communities and individuals that I happen to encounter in my fieldwork: to make an obvious point, it is always me who is present when I observe a religious community. How can I know whether things are different elsewhere in the organisation, or when I am absent? When I attend a meeting, I can only observe those who are present, but what about those who have decided not to attend or who belong to some other congregation?

Insiders and Outsiders

There is a further problem about the bridge of understanding. The model suggests that the scholar and the adherent are on different sides of a bridge, but this is not necessarily the case. Smart's allusion to moccasins will probably alert most of his readers to the unfamiliar nature of many forms of spirituality under study, but what if the reader is an Inuit, to whom moccasin-walking is thoroughly familiar? Increasingly, NRM members write about their own religion; reflexive ethnography is now a well-accredited field in sociology, and autoethnography has become recognised as a legitimate mode of writing about communities.

The 'bridge' metaphor presents an unduly sharp distinction between the researcher and the researched, and presupposes an insider/outsider model of adherence, one which Stephen E. Gregg and I have called into question (Chryssides and Gregg 2019). There are not simply believers and non-believers; there are varying degrees of commitment and non-commitment. NRM members who gain public attention acquire the reputation for having an excess of zeal, since they are often first-generation converts who have joined out of enthusiasm rather than upbringing. However, it would be wrong to suggest that, even in NRMs, this is always the case. Gregg and Chryssides (2017) identified several categories of insider: the rank-and-file member, the long-standing member, and office-bearers with different degrees of centrality in an organisation. There are those who are receiving instruction and working towards membership; contrary to popular belief, NRMs do not welcome everyone, and do not typically grant instant membership. In many cases there is a course of instruction to be followed. For example, the Unification Church used to hold lengthy workshops, often lasting twenty-one days, in which seekers were progressively introduced to the teachings of *Divine Principle*. To become a Jehovah's Witness, one needs to undergo Bible study, which entails studying biblical themes with an instructor, attending congregational meetings, and satisfying the elders on sixty key questions relating to their understanding of the faith, and their lifestyle, after which they become eligible for baptism. At the other end of the spectrum there are those who are wavering about their faith, those who become part of schismatic movements, and those who have become disillusioned. It is not merely in mainstream religions that one finds members who are not totally committed. People may join or remain in a religious organisation for its social function, to keep their marriage together, or simply to attend the occasional event. Ex-members of Jehovah's Witnesses have devised the concept of the 'PIMO', meaning 'Physically In, Mentally Out', designating those who continue to belong to the Watch Tower organisation, but can no longer accept the Society's teachings. They remain inside because the consequences of disassociating would involve being shunned by the rest of the membership – and Jehovah's Witnesses tend to rely on the organisation for their friendships. Exploring all, or at least some, of this complexity is the task of the fieldworker.

Outsiders can fall into various categories. There are those who are simply uninterested, those who maintain an interest in an NRM's affairs, those who decide to follow a schismatic group, and those who are ex-members. As a category, ex-members are not uniform. We tend to hear more from vociferous and hostile ex-members, precisely because they gain publicity for themselves. There is no exact way of determining how representative such ex-members are of the totality of those who leave NRMs, although my own, admittedly inexact, calculation was that there are unlikely to be more than 0.25 per cent of ex-members who were sufficiently negative about their past experience to join an anticult organisation (Gregg and Chryssides 2017: 23). Because most ex-members simply get on with life, they are difficult to locate, precisely because of the low profile that they maintain. Anecdotally, I can recount meeting two such individuals (part of my 'incidental fieldwork'): one had undertaken a short Dianetics course at the Church of Scientology, rated it as 'quite good', but could not afford to undertake further studies; another belonged to the Soka Gakkai, but discontinued after thinking that she was being followed on her way home one night.

The ex-member testimony we hear, therefore, comes from the vociferous leaver, and is not unbiased. Some scholars, such as Lonnie D. Kliever (1995) and Bryan R. Wilson, are inclined to dismiss it entirely. Wilson writes:

> Neither the objective sociological researcher nor the court of law can readily regard the apostate as a creditable or reliable source of evidence. He must

always be seen as one whose personal history predisposes him to bias with respect to both his previous religious commitment and affiliations, the suspicion must arise that he acts from a personal motivation to vindicate himself and to regain his self-esteem, by showing himself to have been first a victim but subsequently to have become a redeemed crusader. As various instances have indicated, he is likely to be suggestible and ready to enlarge or embellish his grievances to satisfy that species of journalist whose interest is more in sensational copy than in a [*sic*] objective statement of the truth. (Wilson 1994: 4; punctuation as original)

James Beckford argues that such ex-members are prone to invent a scenario after leaving the organisation. Possibly embarrassed by the fact that they belonged, and might possibly become victims of prejudice, they want to create some explanation for joining that exonerates themselves from responsibility. They may therefore devise explanations involving deception, brainwashing, or some other involuntary process that suggests that the decision to join was not due to personal choice (Beckford 1978: 112).

Although ex-member testimony must be treated with considerable caution, these assessments should not be accepted uncritically. The ex-member can often gain important insights into the inner workings of an NRM, particularly if he or she has held a position of responsibility. Ex-members have also been known to leak important information which might not otherwise enter the public domain, as occurs notably among former Jehovah's Witnesses and Scientologists. It is also worth noting that Beckford's assessment applies principally to first-generation converts: those who have been brought up within an NRM have been in the community as a result of their upbringing, and have made no personal decision to join that needs to be explained away.

Fieldwork inevitably draws the researcher towards an 'insider' position. One compelling reason for an NRM community to allow the researcher to come in is that members may see him or her as material for conversion. Every so often, my principal Jehovah's Witness informant takes me aside and tells me that he would dearly like me to survive Armageddon, and is concerned that I am 'not yet in the truth'. His counsel invariably includes the phrase 'not yet', which suggests that he believes that there is still some chance that I might be persuaded to become one of their number. The comment implies a degree of spiritual superiority, although it is kindly meant: belonging is something to which I should graduate, and the difference between him and me is not simply theological disagreement. I could reciprocally tell him that he has 'not yet' accepted evolution theory or modern biblical scholarship, but it is a fair assumption that he never will, and engaging in theological argument would not be productive as a means to understanding the Watch Tower organisation. However, 'not-yet-ness' is actually an advantageous position for the researcher. In the unlikely scenario of my coming to accept Watch Tower teachings, I would probably lose credibility in academic circles, and would become a JW spokesperson; it is also likely that my lifestyle could not conform to the congregation's expectations, and I might soon find myself being disfellowshipped. This would of course be a disastrous position for the researcher, since Jehovah's Witnesses are well known for their policy of totally breaking contact with apostates, and my fieldwork would be at an end.

Observing the Negative

As fieldworkers endeavour to adopt an insider's stance, they cannot help bringing to bear elements from their own past outsider position. This need not be a problem if the researcher makes appropriate connections, but this is not always the case. In his study of Jehovah's Witnesses, Andrew Holden writes the following:

> Unlike the Roman Catholic tradition in which relics, crucifixes, statues, pictures, holy water and tabernacles are an indispensable part of the spiritual ethos, the Witnesses' place of worship appears sparse and disenchanted. Throughout the course of my observations, I saw no one meditating or lighting candles and the elders never burned incense. Nor did they wear vestments or stand before an altar. The Hall was essentially functional. (Holden 2002: 65)

Although there is nothing incorrect about Holden's observations, the association between Kingdom Hall meetings and worship in the Roman Catholic tradition seems somehow inappropriate. Commenting on features that one does not find in a religious community can certainly be important, but which should one identify? Jehovah's Witnesses do not light candles, burn incense, or wear vestments, but equally they do not practise infanticide, sky burial, or self-flagellation. It is a legitimate question to consider why certain absent features are worthy of mention but not others. Writing about the first-century Christians, an anonymous author wrote to someone called Diognetus, in which he stated, 'They marry like the rest of the world, they breed children, but they do not cast their offspring adrift' (quoted in Stevenson 1974: 59). It might be appropriate for an author to point out that Zoroastrians in diaspora are unable to practise sky burial, or that some members of Opus Dei do not practise self-flagellation.

When writing about one's fieldwork, it is important to set one's observations within a coherent and meaningful framework, taking into account one's readers' positionality and expectations. Thus it was appropriate for Diognetus' correspondent to mention infanticide, since this was prevalent in Roman society at that time. In a context where readers might have misconceptions about Opus Dei through reading Dan Brown's *The Da Vinci Code*, it is reasonable to correct popularly held misinformation. In the case of Jehovah's Witnesses, it is unlikely that any reader would expect to find these features of Roman Catholicism in a Kingdom Hall, since the Watch Tower Society is historically well separated from the Catholic Church as a result of the Protestant Reformation, and later the Adventist tradition. It might have been more helpful for Holden to identify features that separate Jehovah's Witnesses from Protestantism: his reference to pictures is more apposite, since Witnesses are not opposed to pictorial representations, which feature in the literature, but nonetheless are not found in Kingdom Halls.

Gaining Access

In writing about fieldwork, the scholar is endeavouring to present unfamiliar material to the reader, while relating it to phenomena which he or she will recognise, and which can be meaningfully related to the religion being studied. But, if the scholar is an outsider, how does he or she enter the unfamiliar world of the believer? When H. H. Stroup, who wrote the first serious study of Jehovah's Witnesses in 1945, attempted to start his research by writing to Nathan H. Knorr, the Society's president, he was met with a firm rebuff. Knorr wrote back, saying that the 'Society does not have the time, nor will it take the time, to assist you in your publication concerning Jehovah's witnesses' (Stroup 1945: vi). Knorr's refusal makes the point that religious organisations do not exist as repositories of information for researchers, but rather to encourage their followers' spiritual life and, certainly in the case of Jehovah's Witnesses, to make new converts. Stroup's problem was that he lacked a gate-opener, which is much less of a problem today, now that NRM studies has become an established area of scholarship, and members have become increasingly accustomed to being researched.

Access to religious communities is guarded by two types of person: 'gate-keepers' and 'gate openers'. The term 'gatekeeper' is used widely, in a variety of contexts, denoting those who have the power to control entry and exit, ranging from the bouncer at a nightclub to a royal palace guard. The study of religion is patrolled by various gatekeepers – admissions tutors, examiners, and subsequently those who peer review scholarly journals. In connection with fieldwork, gatekeepers are those who enable researchers to gain access, or prevent them from doing so. The researcher may seek access, either to premises, to events, or to information. Gate openers, on the other hand, are those who are able to facilitate the researcher's access. The gate opener may be one and the same as the gatekeeper, but the difference between the two roles is that the gatekeeper is the official who has authority to allow or prevent access, while the gate opener is the one who provides the opportunity to the researcher, by introducing him or her to the community. The gate opener may not necessarily have an official position, but may simply be a rank-and-file member who can offer a friendly introduction.

Rebuffs such as Knorr's to Stroup are sometimes due to the distrust of a researcher's motives; since there is so much negative literature around about NRMs, it is understandable that their office-bearers fear that the researcher might intend to add to the already voluminous anticult polemic. When I tell Jehovah's Witnesses that I have written books on their organisation, this can create apprehension, rather than appreciation, and I have to make clear that my published writing differs from that of the Protestant evangelicals. Numerous NRMs now tend to be more open to academic research, perceiving that there are advantages in scholarly treatment. They recognise that, in the main, they can rely on scholars to give them fair treatment, and to correct misinformation that is commonly circulated.

If the religious community is one's own, gaining access to the relevant informants is considerably easier, but if one is researching a different faith, it is necessary to find an appropriate point of entry. Entry is not an automatic right, and there are some communities that would be difficult, if not impossible, to penetrate. Someone seeking access to the Exclusive Brethren would encounter serious difficulties, since the organisation prohibits any kind of contact with unbelievers. Gaining entry can happen in several ways: by request from the researcher, by invitation, or by opportunity.

In the world of business, the concept of the gatekeeper connotes a barrier to be surmounted; a quick Google search of the concept swiftly provides websites that offer advice to vendors who need to get past a secretary or receptionist who closely guards the executive to whom they need to speak. The employment of this model in the study of NRMs can be misleading, however, since the gatekeeper is not necessarily a barrier to be overcome, but an important resource for the researcher to use. In many cases the religious community does not present barriers, but positively invites seekers, to the extent of actively reaching out to the wider public. The Mormon missionaries who call at one's door are already entrusted to open their gates to the householders and their families. Indeed, it is the householders, conversely, who become the gatekeepers: they are the ones who decide whether to invite the caller in, and whether to engage with the organisation.

Making formal requests, for example by writing to an organisation's head-quarters, is somewhat like cold calling, and tends to be unproductive, for a variety of reasons. If the organisation's members typically originate from a non-English-speaking country, the recipient may not read English, and it is frequently not the practice of Asian religions to communicate by correspondence. It is unfortunate that universities often insist on formalising relationships between the researcher and the organisation by means of letters of introduction and signed contracts assuring cooperation. These can create barriers rather than facilitate harmonious and productive relationships. Since most religious communities hold events that are open to the public, a rapport is more likely to be established through attending a public gathering, at which access is guaranteed, and which enables relationships with the community to develop naturally. One supervisor I have known recommends that his students simply attend as many gatherings as possible, without any prior agenda, simply to absorb the community's atmosphere and become known to attendees and office-bearers.

Barriers, of course, exist. Andrew Dawson (2010) makes a threefold distinction of how a community might perceive the researcher: he or she may be the 'provisional insider', the 'potential real insider', or the 'counterfeit insider'. The provisional insider is someone who is accepted within the community, at least for the period in which the research is being conducted; the potential real insider is the one who is perceived as a likely candidate for conversion. The third category – the counterfeit insider – is one which the researcher should wish to avoid: it is the situation in which one is regarded as not properly belonging, and perhaps even contaminating the community's purity. (Of course, the researcher may be regarded by different members of the community as falling into different categories.) The researcher's characteristics have a bearing on how he or she is regarded. To be a provisional insider, there must ideally be some commonality between the researcher and the community. In my own work with Jehovah's Witnesses, I have been greatly helped by the fact that I have been brought up in a tradition where I know my Bible reasonably well; my mother was a pacifist and was strongly opposed to smoking and gambling; and she was a regular churchgoer. Despite my lack of rapport with the Watch Tower Society's interpretation of the Bible, at least a common background establishes a common base, and a means of understanding how Witnesses think.

Barriers to Fieldwork

Conversely, there can be personal factors that hinder researching a religious community. In our *The Study of Religion* (2014), Chryssides and Geaves itemise a number of these. One may be seriously hampered by one's religion (or lack of it), gender, ethnicity, sexual orientation, age, language, and sometimes social class. In the case of Hindu and Sikh researchers, caste can sometimes create problems: a Hindu or Sikh researcher can find problems gaining acceptance by members of a community whose caste is higher or lower than the researcher. Being a white male, it is unlikely that I could successfully research a Muslim women's organisation, and a heterosexual researcher might feel out of place in an LGBTQ group. I can recall one situation when I wanted to visit a Seventh-day Adventist (SDA) congregation during an Easter weekend, to find out whether or how they marked this Christian festival. I had not anticipated that the people who were pouring into the church were entirely Black, and that therefore I was going to stand out as being very obviously different. If it had not been for the fact that I would have had to wait an entire year to find the answer to my question, only to encounter the same problem, I would have been strongly tempted to return home. As it turned out, the congregation was extremely welcoming, and even invited me to share in their communal lunch afterwards. The congregation, which I estimated to be about 300-strong, had perhaps half a dozen white members, one of whom appeared to be an office-bearer. SDA founder-leader Ellen G. White (1827–1915) in fact had many contacts with Black communities, and wrote much about slavery and segregation. Black Adventist history merits greater academic attention, and my encounter on that Saturday highlighted a further under-researched area.

A further barrier to research can be financial, a common problem in researching the Church of Scientology, which is well known for the high cost of many of its courses. To progress into the levels of Operating Thetan (OT) the adept can expect to pay thousands of dollars: Donald Westbrook, who has conducted extensive research into Scientology, reports that the average amount mentioned by his interviewees was $207,941 – although it should be emphasised that these were members who were at fairly advanced OT levels, and that such a sum would not be typical of the average supporter (Westbrook 2019: 37).

Gaining access is not necessarily an all-or-nothing matter, since there can be levels of access, and different gatekeepers may be required for different aspects of one's work. In my research on the Unification Church, obtaining access to archives in the London headquarters was a further step beyond attending their seminars. I never managed to attend their daily Pledge service, despite the fact that several of their office-bearers said that this would be an important part of my research. My letter to the UK national president received no reply, although this may have been because he was Japanese and possibly did not read English. During the final seven-day seminar which I attended in 1988, a Pledge service appeared to have taken place without my prior knowledge. The ceremony is typically scheduled for 05:00, and when I got up in the morning at a more reasonable hour, it was evident that the members were emerging from a meeting. It was somewhat puzzling that I should previously have been urged to attend the Pledge, but yet excluded when there was an opportunity. However, since this was a seminar for which members of the public could enrol, they may have taken the view that, since non-members were not invited, they did not wish to make an exception in my case. Faced with lack of permission, the researcher might consider the extent to which a piece of fieldwork was actually necessary. The full text of the Pledge is carefully itemised in the Unification Church's liturgical manual *The Tradition* (Holy Spirit Association 1985), so I am unsure whether attending would have added anything significant. I have subsequently attempted to find versions on YouTube, but these do not portray members in traditional robes, as the manual instructs, and appear to be designed for private devotional purposes. Of course, such adaptations are themselves of interest to researcher, as is the fact that I was excluded: as Eileen Barker once commented, 'Everything is data' (Palmer 2004:12).

Dress Codes and the Role of Photography

Appropriate dress and demeanour are a *sine qua non* for the fieldworker. Although one might not necessarily be excluded from attending an event when inappropriately dressed, it is an important part of the researcher's attempt to be unobtrusive in the role of the provisional insider, and compliance demonstrates appropriate prior knowledge of the community, and is conducive to securing acceptance. How far one takes adapting one's appearance can be a matter of judgement. For example, beards have not been favoured among Jehovah's Witnesses in the West, although not totally prohibited, but a male researcher blends in better if clean-shaven. My own attempts at conforming to expectations go as far as cleaning my car before visiting a Kingdom Hall, since attendees' vehicles are invariably immaculate.

Gaining access is not unconditional or unlimited. The Daesoon Jinrihoe – a Korean new religious movement – do not allow visitors to go beyond the *Sungdomun* Gate – the entrance to the *Jeongnae* (interior court) – unless clad in traditional Korean attire (*hanbok*), or business suits as an alternative for men. Visitors are asked to maintain a solemn and reverent attitude throughout, and not to wander around the courtyard. At the entrance one faces the *Bonjeon* Hall, which is the most sacred part of the complex, and consists of four storeys. The second and third floors contain sacred paintings (*Daesoon Seongjeon*), and at the top is the *Yeongdae*, which houses images of the Supreme God Kang Jeungsan, together with fourteen other principal deities. On ascending the stairs, visitors are required to adopt the *Myeonsu* posture, which involves bowing one's head and having one's hands crossed over one's abdomen. While these may seem complex requirements, partly designed to deter the over-casual sightseer, Daesoon Jinrihoe positively encourages visitors, and will arrange a temple stay to introduce them to their spiritual life and to Korean culture (Daesoon Jinrihoe 2023). Gatekeeping is therefore somewhat more nuanced than that of the company receptionist or the nightclub bouncer.

Daesoon Jinrihoe temples also have strict rules regarding photography. While one may take photographs in the outer court area, photography is disallowed once the visitor has entered the interior court. The role of photography tends to receive relatively little mention in discussions of fieldwork in religion, but it is a valuable tool that should not be neglected. Pictures provide a more permanent record of a field visit, and not only reactivate one's memories, but can retrospectively show details of religious premises or events which the researcher may not have noticed at the time. Photographing signage and information panels can also reduce the task of note-taking. Since modern cameras, and even the camera facility on many smartphones, can be quite powerful, a photograph can often reveal hidden details that may not initially be physically visible to the researcher. This is particularly the case when photographing objects at a distance or, where flash photography is permitted, one can subsequently view details of a location that is too dark to be seen. Maintaining a photo library also has the function of highlighting changes that are made to religious premises as time progresses. The researcher–photographer can also home in on details that he or she finds particularly significant, but which might not normally form part of a commercial photograph. Commercial photography, particularly in coffee-table books, frequently sanitises its subject matter, preferring physical attractiveness to authenticity, typically removing items such as donation boxes or fortune-telling devices in temples, which are judged either to be visually unattractive, or which detract from an idealised version that the authors seek to portray. Although the Aryan symbol of the swastika is frequently found in Hindu and Buddhist temples, it is rarely to be seen in popular commercial publications.

Many religious communities are becoming reluctant to allow photography, however. At times, the reasons can be commercial and pragmatic: acquiring one's own photograph can cause a gift shop to forfeit a sale, and photographing people might invade their privacy. Flash photography, if permitted over a prolonged period, can cause damage to pictures and artefacts. The proliferation of smartphones with camera facilities has given rise to increased photography, and unfortunately this has caused a growing number of religious communities to prohibit it completely. Not only is camera noise a distraction to worshippers, but it can be viewed as irreverent: tourists who take selfies in front of a buddha rupa must turn their back to the image, which many Buddhists would find insulting. There are also issues of security. Particularly with the increasing tendency to display one's pictures on social media, criminals can discover where valuable artefacts are housed, and visual information about the layout of a building can facilitate their activities. There can also be religious objections to photography. The SGI's gohonzon is regarded as too sacred to be captured in a photograph, while in other traditions, a *murti* is believed to contain the divine, and devotees believe that it might lose its energy by being captured on camera. Indeed, photography can be regarded as a form of disguised kidnapping. (We talk about 'taking' a photograph, as if the object forfeits something through photography.)

It can be tempting to sneak an illicit photograph, or switch on an audio-recorder, but religious communities have a right to privacy and to set their rules. The researcher lies within a different category from the tourist or the worshipper, although it is sometimes possible for the gatekeeper to give a special dispensation to serious students who are not simply wanting souvenirs. At the Ek Niwas Universal Divine Temple in Wolverhampton, UK, despite the prominent 'No photography' sign at the entrance, the resident baba has invariably given me and accompanying students permission to photograph any part of the worship area.

Power Relationships

The relationship between researchers and the community's gatekeepers and gate-openers is a kind of power relationship. The gatekeepers have the power to determine what access might be given to scholars, what events they might attend, and what literature should be made accessible. Reciprocally, scholars have the power to decide what information to disseminate, and how they present their material. But should the researcher go beyond fair and accurate coverage, and allow members of the community to see one's work in progress, and to suggest possible changes? Much depends on the relationships we have built up with our informants. Jehovah's Witnesses have invariably been amenable to reading and discussing my own work, as a result of which I have been able to make improvements and at times corrections, and their scrutiny has always been on the understanding that I am the final arbiter of what appears in the text. I have not always accepted their preferred amendments, and this has not damaged relationships. On the other hand, I have encountered organisations that have put pressure on me to omit sections of my text, or have set unreasonable conditions for using their material in an anthology; as a consequence, I no longer offer them the opportunity for prior viewing.

Sometimes expectations go further than wishing to see the text in advance of publication, and an organisation may at times request support from scholars.

This can involve being asked to write letters to politicians, or supportive statements for their own webpages and publications. How one treats such requests is a matter of judgement, and one must decide whether the cause is just, and whether one's intervention is likely to be effective. I have been happy to write statements that can be found on the JW.org website concerning the persecution of Jehovah's Witnesses in Russia, as have several other researchers in the field (Watch Tower 2020). Their treatment has been obviously unjust, and the repercussions for simply being a Jehovah's Witness are totally deplorable. By contrast, some Scientologists once asked me to write to Google, protesting that its algorithms were unfair, since searching the word 'Scientology' invariably put the web user in touch with their detractors. On that occasion, I declined, since I have no knowledge about how algorithms work in cyberspace, and cannot adjudicate on their appropriateness or otherwise. One should not support causes that one does not understand.

4 Collecting and Analysing Data

Most readers will be familiar with the various methods of data collection: observation, participant–observation, formal interviews, questionnaires, keeping journals, the use of audio and video recording, and researching on the Internet (which will be dealt with in Section 6). When researching religious communities, simple observation is difficult. If some event is taking place, I become part of the action as soon as I cross the threshold, and look out of place if I cannot behave like the regular members by being inappropriately dressed, lacking any necessary requisites, or not knowing when to stand up, sit down, or make appropriate movements. The fieldwork researcher's position is often described as liminality. Unless engaged in reflexive ethnography, the researcher is on the boundaries, adopting the role of the insider as far as is feasible, without being part of the community. Before attending a Kingdom Hall meeting, my own practice is to ascertain what songs will be used and to try to learn them in advance, in order to be able to participate as fully as possible. This information frequently can be found online, but not all religious organisations provide such detailed data.

The degree of proximity to the boundaries is a matter of judgement for the researcher. Notwithstanding the desirability of conformity, fieldwork researchers have their own identity to maintain. Being a vegetarian researching an omnivorous community, for example, poses an obvious dilemma. Does one require the community to make special concessions, or does one abandon one's dietary principles and conform in order to experience the phenomenon as it is? In his study *The Beggar in Sri Lanka* (1979) Nandasēna Ratnapāla decided to abandon his vegetarianism and eat meatballs like other beggars. This was a piece of covert research, however, and maintaining his principles would no doubt have blown his cover. Conversely, I have known evangelical Christian students who declined to accept food at Hindu-related organisations like ISKCON, on the grounds that they believe the food had been offered to idols (1 Corinthians 8:1–8). In the Unification Church, members will characteristically bow in front of the picture of Sun Myung Moon and his wife Hak Ja Han. I have personally never found myself able to do this, although I can understand other researchers who might feel that complying with such a custom is no more than a perfunctory physical gesture.

Those who have their own religion can devise ways of compromising with what they feel uncomfortable. When Unificationist lecturers were systematically explaining *Divine Principle*, they asked the audience questions like, 'What qualifications must the messiah have?' Faced with such a question, I could have answered it from my own mainstream Christian perspective, but that would not have been productive in attempting to understand Unificationist teaching, and might simply have provoked an adversarial argument. My tactic was to explain to the lecturer that, as a non-Unificationist, I might feel constrained to give answers that differed from the expected ones, but in the interests of gaining understanding I would supply the answers that I thought would be expected from a seeker undergoing such instruction. Both the lecturer and I were happy with this arrangement, and thus the seminar could proceed, enhancing my own understanding while avoiding theological confrontation. On other occasions, compliance may be undesirable. One of my postgraduate students researching the New Age in Russia joined a group that proposed performing a New Age dance in the grounds of an Orthodox monastery. While it might have been interesting to let them proceed and observe the consequences, she rightly dissuaded them. The Eastern Orthodox churches do not take kindly to other forms of religion, particularly NRMs and New Age, and there might well have been arrests. Personal safety, obedience to the law of the land, and respect for sacred spaces can be considerations that militate against participant–observation.

Questionnaires and Interviews

Devising questionnaires and organising interviews can be important for collecting data. In researching NRMs there are obvious problems in identifying appropriate participants. Some researchers have advertised for volunteers, but this can readily result in a biased sample. The vociferous ex-member is more likely to respond than an ordinary rank-and-file member or someone who has left for unremarkable mundane reasons. Where researchers have employed snowball sampling in order to increase the number of participants, members of the initial sample are prone to find like-minded acquaintances, rather than people who might present a divergent viewpoint. Although undergraduates whom I have taught have often been keen to utilise their interviewing skills, in many cases studies already exist, and Internet sites like the Pew Forum have already amassed data, operating on a scale that the average researcher would find impossible.

There are other problems about interviews that are not so commonly acknowledged. Interviews are frequently episodic single events, and typically formal. Members of one NRM reported to me that they had previously undergone interviews by a well-known and well-accredited researcher, and that some of them had felt nervous in the presence of such a high-profile academic. This power imbalance is not only inherently a matter of concern: a nervous interviewee is less likely to give good coherent information, and interviewees may give answers that they think the interviewer wants, rather than what they genuinely think. They do not typically have the opportunity to reconsider the responses, or they may not elaborate beyond what the interviewer asks. Interviews, of course, have the advantage that the material can be recorded and transcribed, ensuring that the interviewer has the interviewee's exact wording – although the use of recording devices can itself contribute to an interviewee's nervousness. The process of coding responses can ensure that analysis of the respondent's words is scientific and reliable, and that the researcher has not cherry-picked remarks that are amenable to his or her thesis.

'Going Native' and 'Living In'

Closer acquaintance with NRMs is achieved by living with a community for an extended period of time. Anthropologists have sometimes referred to this method as 'going native', a term which Andrew Holden (2002: 4), taking his cue from Malinowski, uses to describe his research into a Jehovah's Witnesses congregation in Blackburn. The term 'going native' is sometimes regarded as pejorative, suggesting that the community being studied is backward or uneducated. Also, if going native suggests that the researcher has adopted all of the community's practices, this is not always possible or desirable. Holden does not tell us whether, like most practising Witnesses, he carried a 'no blood' card, whether he said grace before meals, or invariably studied the set *Watchtower* articles. Of course, not all members practise in the same way, and they have different degrees of commitment, so there is no reason why a researcher should attempt to replicate the lifestyle of the ideal member exactly. One might also question whether it is necessary for a researcher to adopt all of a community's practices in order to research it effectively.

Less pejorative is the term 'living in', which is sometimes employed to describe the position of a researcher who maintains extended contact with an intentional community – the sociological term for a residential community that occurs deliberately rather than accidentality. Notable examples have included the Unification Church, The Family International, and ISKCON in the 1970s and 1980s (see, e.g., Mickler 2022; Borowik 2023; Burt 2023). Perhaps more frequently, researchers are in a position where they live outside the community in close proximity and commute in order to participate in significant events. Intentional communities are on the decline, since in many cases community living became incompatible with members' changing lifestyle. The Unification Church defined three different categories of membership in the 1980s: full-time (residential) membership, home church membership, and associate membership. The Family International is no longer community-based but is now predominantly a publishing house, although members may, if they wish, continue to adopt old-style community living. Others only allow community membership for certain purposes: Jehovah's Witnesses' 'Bethels' – regional headquarters for the production and dissemination of their literature – only allow brief overnight stays by family members. Apart from residents at its Celebrity Centers, Scientologists tend to live near their 'org', and the LDS Church allows residential accommodation for missionary training and members who come to a temple to perform endowments. For a short period, my students were allowed to stay overnight in the London Mormon Temple's accommodation for members who came to receive endowments, and on one occasion I was assigned a room reserved for the President. However, staff changes at their Missionary Training Centre unfortunately ended this generous permission. The researcher is therefore more likely to be in the position of a regular attendee, who commutes from home or find temporary nearby accommodation when this is needed.

The Fieldworker as 'Guest'

Graham Harvey's (2003a) notion of the researcher as 'guest', I believe, best encapsulates the role of the fieldworker. The concept arises from Harvey's fieldwork among the Māori in New Zealand, which he also uses in his research on modern Paganism. He argues that the guest analogy is preferable to the description 'going native', which he regards as colonialist. Harvey perceives guest status as a middle position between a collaborator and an opponent. From the Māori perspective, anyone who does not belong to the community is viewed as a stranger, who might be either a friend or an enemy. In order to enter the community's compound, a number of protocols must be observed, in which the stranger must be formally invited. However, the stranger always remains a guest, since belonging to the community depends on ancestry and permanently excludes the researcher from complete belonging.

Although participant–observation in a religious community does not usually involve such formalised steps, the analogy of the guest is useful in understanding one's ideal relationship with spiritual groups with which one typically remains the outsider. A good household guest is there by invitation, and recognises that the hosts have their expectations of their visitors. Good guests recognise the boundaries to observe: there are physical boundaries to respect, such as the hosts' bedroom; there are expected forms of behaviour; and there are activities for which the hosts' permission should be sought. Similarly, in researching NRMs – or indeed any community – the researcher must accept that there may be places which are out of bounds, material that is confidential, and activities to which one may not gain access. Sometimes an NRM's detractors will allege that an organisation keeps secret files – put this way, it makes the movement sound sinister. Yet many mainstream religious groups have information that is to be kept confidential, such as congregational directories, data on members' financial contributions, minutes of meetings, and records of counselling sessions.

Data Contamination

One key concern of the ethnographer is the avoidance of data contamination. The fieldworker should seek to observe and portray the phenomenon as it is, and disrupt it as little as possible. However, various factors may hinder accurate portrayal of the community being studied. The very fact of my presence means that I am studying the community with myself within it, unlike the photographer who remains outside the photograph. Data contamination may come from the NRM itself, whose members are naturally keen to portray the organisation in as favourable a light as possible. At worst, this may take the form of members telling deliberate untruths, while more commonly NRMs may provide material for public relations rather than show their usual practice. Particularly if the researcher's presence is anticipated by the community, deliberate changes may be made in their practice in order to gain a more favourable assessment from the fieldworker.

Other forms of data contamination may come from researchers themselves, as Elisabeth Arweck points out (Arweck and Stringer 2002: 115–32). Researchers want to be able to continue their fieldwork, and may fear that providing unduly negative information would lead to their exclusion. Benefits such as hospitality, or even receiving payment, may lead the researcher to emphasise the organisation's positive aspects at the expense of more negative ones. An organisation that offers expenses-paid conferences, involving foreign travel and additional field visits, is likely to cause scholars to gravitate towards it, to the exclusion of rival groups that do not offer such benefits. More negatively, fear of litigation has been an inhibiting factor to some scholars, who would not wish to be involved in a libel suit, even if their information was sound.

How Far Should One Go?

Participation can sometimes occasion changes in the movement being researched. Eriko Kawanishi, a Japanese scholar who specialises in New Age studies, with particular reference to Glastonbury, England, attended the 2009 Goddess Conference. The organiser asked her to perform an Amaterasu Dance as part of the event. Kawanishi pointed out that there is no such dance, and she drew attention to numerous misapprehensions among the Glastonbury New Agers about Japanese culture and mythology. In the Amaterasu myth, Usume, a different Japanese goddess, performs a dance in which she exposes her naked body, which of course would have been inappropriate both for the Goddess community and for the researcher. The organiser suggested that Kawanishi might devise an Amaterasu Dance of her own and perform it to their audience. Since this organiser and other members of the community had previously been helpful to her research, she felt she could not decline, so she invented an inauthentic dance, which she preceded by explaining the real story of Amaterasu. Some years later a member of the audience to which Kawanishi performed organised a workshop on Amaterasu as sacred drama. As Kawanishi states, 'In fact, my performance had not ended in 2009, but lasted in the memories of those who witnessed it and influenced their re-creations of the myth' (Kawanishi 2021: 172). Clearly Kawanishi took the view that, since the researcher inevitably changes the phenomenon, she could legitimately become part of the phenomenon under research, and influence the direction that the movement takes.

In her research on Haitan Vodou, Karen McCarthy Brown (1991) writes autobiographically about her relationship with Mama Lola, a Vodou priestess in Brooklyn. Brown describes how she met Mama Lola and recounts their conversations, as well as their agreement to split book royalties equally with her informant. She goes on to divulge details to the priestess about her personal life, including her divorce, for which she seeks and accepts her guidance.

Mama Lola recommended that she should undergo a ritual, in which she became spiritually married to Papa Ogou, a spirit who was Mama Lola's guide and counsellor.

As Brown acknowledges, her relationship with Mama Lola was so intimate that effectively she had converted to Vodou, and subsequently felt the need to disengage. She writes:

> As Alourdes [Mama Lola] and I became friends, I found it increasingly difficult to maintain an uncluttered image of myself as scholar and researcher in her presence. This difficulty brought about a change in the research I was doing. As I got closer to Alourdes, I got closer to Vodou. The Vodou Alourdes practices is intimate and intense, and I soon found that I could not claim a place in her Vodou family and remain a detached observer. (Brown 1991: 9)

There are instances where one might question whether there is a distinction between researcher and practitioner. Modern Druidry does not characteristically have defined beliefs, agreed scriptures, or distinctive codes of ethics, but involves the celebration of eight seasonal festivals. By participating in these, one might ask whether the field researcher is in a different position from the practitioners. The distinction between practitioner and researcher can at times be blurred. From time to time researchers may feel that they are gaining spiritual development through acquaintance with their subject matter. This no doubt gives added empathy, but it may be at the expense of critical distance.

Accepting Hospitality

I commended the fieldworker's role as the guest. Frequently, researchers take the initiative in asking to be invited inside NRMs, which would be normally regarded as a breach of protocol in conventional interpersonal relationships. However, some NRMs have positively taken the initiative in attracting scholars to the organisation. In the 1980s and early 1990s, a variety of associations sponsored by Sun Myung Moon's Unification Movement invited large numbers of academics, clergy, and sometimes politicians to events in various parts of the world, paying for their travel and accommodation. Some of these events were about the Unification Church's teachings, but most were about religious and societal themes. These events inevitably proved controversial for several reasons. The Unification Church was perceived as courting academics, perhaps in the hope of gaining legitimacy, and securing support when needed. Many invitees declined the invitation, and some of the organisation's guests had reservations, partly on the grounds that Moon was convicted of tax fraud in 1982 (although some believed that his prison sentence was unjust), and partly because a proportion of their finances were raised by young converts who worked long hours with their mobile fundraising teams. Other organisations have paid academics to attend their special events, and most recently the Korean NRM, Daesoon Jinrihoe, has invited selected academics to South Korea to give presentations at their own proceedings, sometimes offering fees to presenters as well as complimentary board and travel.

It can be argued that such invitations are cynical attempts to gain credibility, and that attendees will find it difficult to maintain critical distance when they are indebted to organisations that have offered generous hospitality. They can also have the effect of enabling those outside the organisation to help to develop its theology. Currently the Daesoon Jinrihoe sponsors the *Journal of the Daesoon Academy of Sciences* which, unusually, pays contributors, and offers an enhanced fee for those who write about Daesoon Jinrihoe. On the one hand, sympathisers can argue that these international conferences are part of the NRM phenomenon, and that attendance can be justified in the name of research. On the other hand, helping to develop and promote a community's theology is arguably disturbing the phenomenon, rather than leaving it as it is. There is a further consideration: apart from such issues, an organisation that promotes such events is giving itself prominence over similar organisations that offer no such benefits. Although Daesoon Jinrihoe is said to be the largest NRM in Korea, it is one of many similar organisations, and the legitimacy of its founder–leader Park Wundang (1918–1996) is disputed. Its sponsorship of these affairs privileges its attention by academics over the other rival organisations, which may be more difficult to research without appropriate funding.

Writing about NRMs

The word 'ethnography' literally means writing about people, and an ethnographer is therefore not someone who merely undertakes fieldwork by talking to members of the community, but someone who also writes about them. As Gary Alan Fine (1993) points out, the field researcher's work is largely backstage. Few people see us participating in the activities about which we write, and few have access to our field notes. The researcher is therefore largely taken on trust, and if we create errors, these typically remain undetected, and can be replicated by those who read our accounts. Although NRMs have their own gatekeepers, when it comes to writing about groups, the scholar is the gatekeeper of the information he or she has acquired. We can decide which aspects to present, what to include, and what to omit.

Fieldworkers like to present themselves as honest, observant, fair, yet candid, but Fine argues that such ideals are at best problematic. He has provocatively entitled his article 'Ten Lies about Ethnography', by which he means biases that we have and illusions that we can create. Fine is writing about ethnography in general, rather than NRMs specifically, but his argument is certainly relevant to NRM fieldwork. He identifies ten characteristics that the ethnographer endeavours to present as a self-image. These include qualities like kindliness, honesty, being observant, unobtrusiveness, and fairness. However, as he argues, in reality there are numerous factors which compromise these virtues. I might present myself as favourably disposed to an NRM, perhaps because it is unduly maligned in the press, or because I wish to return kindnesses that have been shown, or perhaps I have ulterior motives such as collecting further data, or receiving benefits such as invitations to desirable locales. This may cause me to present an unduly favourable picture of the organisation in question, and I may overlook negative features or misleading – or even false – information that I might be given. While attempting to practise honesty, I cannot claim to have made full disclosure of my data. This is impossible, since an article or even an extended monograph cannot include everything, and I have to select my material. The very act of selection creates bias, and may be done in order to confirm a theory I wish to champion.

Fine also draws attention to the researcher's technical skills. I might regard myself as observant and unobtrusive, and providing a precise account of an event or a conversation I have had with members. However, my observations may be skewed by what I decide to observe, and my powers of observation are not perfect, possibly causing me to miss data that should have been apparent. What I observe is also selective, either intentionally or inadvertently. Inexperienced undergraduates frequently have problems about identifying which observations to report when undertaking fieldwork, sometimes commenting on the colour of the walls, or the precise length of a sermon. Popper's comment that one cannot simply observe, but must direct one's observations to a specific goal is apposite here (see Section 1).

Fine also comments about precision. The fieldworker's ideal is that his or her work should be precise and accurate. However, recording and retrieving our data can be difficult. Visibly taking notes can make the researcher stand out as different, and appear impolite. Making audio recordings can be perceived as an intrusion, and many religious communities disallow using video or audio devices. In the case of Jehovah's Witnesses, however, note-taking is not so much a problem, since attendees are encouraged to take notes, and even train young children to attempt to do so. However, as Fine points out, most researchers are not stenographers, nor possess the ability to write in shorthand; hence, we cannot guarantee that we have captured everything that was important. Moreover, taking notes or producing a recording device during an interview can create barriers, and can make the interviewee unduly self-conscious.

Fine concludes that the ethnographer creates the 'illusion of verisimilitude', but cannot guarantee exact precision.

Fine's article is deliberately provocative, and his critique might suggest that writing about one's fieldwork is worthless. However, various techniques exist to enable the researcher to surmount the problems Fine identifies. One course of action is to formalise the process of interviewing by overtly seeking permission to record responses, then transcribing them, identifying various recurrent themes, and coding the text of the transcription. This arguably makes one's work more scientific and reliable, although there is still scope for subjectivity within the coding process. A further strategy for ensuring greater accuracy is to be accompanied on field visits; one can discuss one's experience with an associate, who can corroborate or correct one's observations, and point out aspects that one may have missed. Again, one can check one's material with one's informants. As the scholar of religion William Cantwell Smith wrote, 'no statement about a religion is valid unless it can be acknowledged by that religion's believers' (Smith, qtd. in Eliade and Kitagawa 1959: 42). It should be noted that Smith used the word 'acknowledged' rather than 'accepted'. The adherent's account of his or her religion need not necessarily be privileged over the scholar's. Adherents may get things wrong, they may fail to recognise scholarly jargon, or they may wish certain aspects of their faith not to be mentioned. Nonetheless, they can point out the researcher's errors, omissions, or unwarranted bias, which must be taken seriously. One informant once mentioned to me that his community did not use the expression 'rites of passage', suggesting that this was inappropriate; he was unfamiliar with the difference between emic and etic vocabulary.

Although we strive for accuracy and precision, the pursuit of these virtues is a quest for the impossible. We are not infallible, we cannot include everything, and we cannot satisfy adherents, critics, and other scholars simultaneously. The study of religion is not an exact science, and scholars should be assured by Aristotle's observation:

> For it is the mark of an educated mind to expect that amount of exactness in each kind which the nature of the particular subject admits. It is equally unreasonable to accept merely probable conclusions from a mathematician and to demand strict demonstration from an orator. (Aristotle, *Nicomachean Ethics*, I.4, 1094b)

5 Ethical Considerations

The interest in formulating codes of practice began as a result of the human experiments conducted on Jews under the Third Reich, which led to the 1946

Declaration of Helsinki, approved by the World Medical Assembly. The key points in the Declaration are that one's research should be sound, conducted by appropriately qualified researchers, with due regard for the privacy of one's subjects. Participants should be given an explanation of the nature of the research, its methods, and its anticipated benefits and potential risks, and should be invited to give informed consent, with the explanation that they may abstain or withdraw from any aspect of the research project at any time, without necessarily having to explain the reasons. The Declaration also stipulated that research should be scrutinised by an ethics committee, with reference to a defined code of practice (World Medical Organization 1996).

Since then, there has been a proliferation of codes of practice spanning a variety of subject areas. A code of practice does not usually have legal status, although compliance and non-compliance may be used in law courts to determine responsibility. Codes of practice differ from codes of ethics, which have existed from ancient times, particularly among religions, which almost invariably have their own ethical dimensions. Examples of the latter include the Noahide Covenant, the Ten Commandments, the Eightfold Path of Buddhism, the Golden Rule in all of its variants, and rules of life that are binding on members of monastic communities. Researchers whose participant–observation work involves living in will normally be expected to abide by such rules. Codes of practice differ in that they are formulated, not by the religious communities themselves, but by bodies representing a wide range of professions, defining good and bad practice, and serving to regulate their members. University ethics committees and grant-awarding bodies will now normally require an assurance that those seeking approval or research funding demonstrate an awareness of and compliance with their relevant code of practice.

Some codes have sought to define acceptable practice across a range of disciplines, for example the Concordat to Support Research Integrity in the United Kingdom, first published in 2012, and revised in 2022 (Universities UK 2022). The Concordat seeks to define acceptable research practice across all subject areas, and its principles are therefore generic rather than specific. It itemised five components of research integrity: honesty, rigour, transparency and open communication, care and respect, and accountability. It also identified a number of unacceptable practices, notably fabrication and falsification of data, plagiarism, and failure to meet legal, ethical, and professional obligations. It also stipulated that institutions should have methods of dealing with allegations of academic misconduct. Ranging over such a wide range of subject areas, inevitably the Concordat defines a common denominator, rather than making subject-specific recommendations.

The study of religion was somewhat slower than other fields to formulate its own codes of practice. The American Academy of Religion (AAR)'s statement of acceptable practice was published in 2016. This was somewhat later than the American Sociological Association Code of Ethics in 1970 (ASA 2023), and the American Anthropological Association Code of Ethics (1998), which were used previously by scholars of religion, since sociology and anthropology were cognate disciplines. Before the formulation of its code, the AAR addressed problems relating to sexual harassment and LGBTQ issues, but its statement of Responsible Research Practices now embraces free enquiry, respect for diversity, fairness and honesty, and the preservation and disclosure of evidence, among other issues that impinge on fieldwork.

In the United Kingdom the Association of University Departments of Theology and Religious Studies (AUDTRS, now subsumed within the Higher Education Academy) published a Framework of Professional Practice in 2005. The working party that produced the document took the view that ethical issues did not have agreed answers, and that they should do no more than identify the various stakeholders whose interests should be considered by researchers when making ethical decisions. Although this position has some merit, the British Association for the Study of Religions subsequently took the view that they did not offer sufficient guidance to be acceptable to university committees and grant-awarding bodies, and that a more definitive statement about ethics should be forthcoming. A revised document entitled 'Ethical Guidelines' underwent various drafts, and was finally accepted in 2019.

This statement sought to be realistic about ethics. It is very easy to state that as scholars of religion we are committed to confidentiality, honesty, openness and transparency, equality, and avoidance of harm, but there are problems in applying these principles to field research in religious organisations. It is unfortunate that universities tend to adopt a one-size-fits-all approach to every research project, irrespective of the area of research and its methodology. The biomedical model essentially applies to research on the human body that is potentially invasive. Most participants in medical research or treatment would certainly want to give consent before being injected with syringes or being participants in a pioneering drugs trial. However, research on NRMs does not involve any kind of invasiveness to the research environment; on the contrary, the researcher seeks to ensure that the phenomena under investigation are left as they are. Whether religious organisations should consent to being researched is a debatable point. If they do not wish our presence at an event, the gatekeepers are in a position to ensure this, and it is often difficult to determine who should give consent, if one's institution expects evidence of authorisation. In the case of Jehovah's Witnesses, it is difficult to ascertain who should be approached.

One might try the chairman of the elders (which is a position that rotates annually), or the Circuit Overseer, or the branch office, but their names are not normally in the public domain, and any correspondence tends to be answered by the Watch Tower Bible and Tract Society's impersonal stamp, rather than an identifiable individual. However, Jehovah's Witnesses' meetings are open to the public, which itself should be sufficient indication that a researcher's presence is not unwelcome. At large events, with as many as 9,000 attendees or more, it would be impossible to secure general agreement, or even to let anyone know that a researcher was present.

In some cases, seeking consent may be sufficient to prevent important research from getting off the ground. If one is researching a far-right group, for example, its members may not welcome the presence of a researcher. Nonetheless, it may well be important for a scholar to undertake fieldwork, in order to disseminate information that is potentially in the public interest. Such examples present a compelling case for covert research.

Current university practice also implies that researchers have satisfied ethical requirements at the outset of the research, whereas fieldwork can present ethical issues that have not been anticipated. The current system of obtaining ethical approval tends to be adversarial, with ethics approval tending to be construed as overcoming an obstacle. 'I've done my ethics!' is something one sometimes hears, with the possible implication that no further ethical issues need to be considered. In the current climate, the ethics committees set themselves up as the authority, as if their members knew better than the individual researcher, despite the fact that many of their members have not studied ethics formally, and have had no training in the subject. Frequently they are dominated by scientists, engineers, and accountants, whose subjects certainly raise ethical issues, but ones that are substantially different from those encountered in the study of religion. In one university to which I belonged, only two members of its ethics committee, out of around two dozen, had any formal qualifications in ethics. The situation would be much improved if ethics committees could act as mentors and offer support and advice to researchers on the ethical dilemmas that they faced, instead of creating hurdles for researchers to overcome. It could also profitably be recognised that, while certain practices are clearly unethical, ethical decisions are frequently controversial, and there can be no agreed answers: researchers may at times have to exercise their own consciences. Murray Dyck and Gary Allen (2013) suggest that it is possible for ethics committees themselves to act unethically. Although writing in the context of medical ethics, their argument equally applies to fieldwork research in the study of religion. They point out that ethics committees frequently subject applicants to inordinate delays, abuse power relationships in the way they pass judgement on students' work, and disregard the integrity of researchers by disallowing them the right to make their own ethical judgements.

The delays imposed by the system of gaining ethics approval cause researchers to be obliged to wait until a committee meets, which may be as infrequently as twice in a semester. This is a hopeless situation when decisions need to be made swiftly. One morning I received a telephone call from my principal informant in the local Jehovah's Witnesses' congregation, who enquired if I had ever attended a Kingdom Hall funeral, and asked if I would like to come to one that was taking place that afternoon. I can imagine an ethics committee having a field day adjudicating on such an invitation! Since I could see no ethical objection to attending, and did not wish to wait until I received a subsequent invitation (which may not have been forthcoming), I hastily put on my suit and tie and made my way to the Kingdom Hall. It would have been more reprehensible to pass up the opportunity to fill in an important gap in my fieldwork. I do not think I subsequently reported my attendance to any ethics committee, although others may think I should have done so.

A further issue frequently raised by ethics committees relates to the storage of data, where again a biomedical model of research is typically assumed. Certainly it is important to ensure that field notes, particularly when informants are identifiable, do not fall into the wrong hands. Universities often require one's research files to be stored under lock and key; however, at two recent conferences at which participants were given student accommodation, the desk drawers had no locks, making compliance impossible. Susan Palmer comments on one university's requirement to destroy data after seven years (Palmer 2017: 254). Again, such a policy might be appropriate for some medical records, but it would create a serious barrier to researchers who might wish to undertake a diachronic study of an NRM, spanning a longer period.

Limits to Integrity?

Although field researchers may like to think that they can foster an environment of integrity, transparency, and equality, the religions we study, by their very nature, often present limits to such ideals. Many new religious movements – and indeed many traditional ones – do not promote equality, for example by disallowing women to hold certain offices, or denying them access to certain parts of their premises on account of their gender. One such example is the Ek Niwas Universal Divine Temple in Wolverhampton, in which the mediaeval Hindu saint Balak Nath is revered. There is a shrine which is called the *guffa* (cave) – a model cave which contains an image of Balak Nath, together with attendants – which sits on a raised balcony, which can be accessed by climbing a few steps. There is a notice that states firmly that women may not climb the steps to where Balak Nath stands. The reason for the prohibition is not that women are regarded as inferior, but rather that Balak Nath was a celibate ascetic, and it would be disrespectful for him (and, by extension, his *murti,* or image) to be in close proximity to women. In actual fact, most of the shrine can be seen from ground level, but on student field visits I have offered to photograph the *murti* on their behalf.

Of course, it is not always a man's world in the study of religion. Until the twenty-first century men were not allowed to enter the Goddess Temple in Glastonbury in England, and researching women's communities cannot readily be undertaken by men. Political correctness is not always a feature of NRMs – or indeed traditional religions – and as students of religion our task is to note and explain it, rather than try to correct it. By secular Western standards, numerous spiritual communities are sexist, racist, and homophobic. Whether they should be given a platform or permitted to distribute their literature may be determined by one's institutional policy, but it would be inappropriate to exclude them from academic study simply because their values clash with institutional equal opportunities policies.

Some Ethical Dilemmas

The values of the Concordat to Support Research Integrity – honesty, rigour, transparency, respect, and accountability – may seem axiomatic, but are there situations where such values are not wholly applicable? In may be appropriate here to recount some occasions where I have had genuine ethical dilemmas, which might seem to go against the high principles that are defined by those who formulate these codes of practice. I leave readers to decide whether I acted rightly or wrongly, or whether their decision would have been different. The first example involved my early years of researching the Unification Church. The organisation presented me with two articles in magazines published by a Pentecostal denomination, which recounted that an early Unification Church leader had studied in Wales, and made contact with one of their congregations. Having told them about the Holy Spirit Association for the Unification of World Christianity (its official name), the Unificationist impressed the congregation, to the extent that they contacted their denomination's branch in Australia, which sent out one of their missionaries to meet Sun Myung Moon and other early supporters in Korea. The articles implied that the missionary welcomed the Unificationists' work, and that they established a good rapport. The relationship sounded somewhat strange, and I wanted to check on the veracity of these reports. I wrote to the Welsh congregation's secretary, giving precise references to the publications, and received a somewhat curt reply, stating that he had searched their records and could not find the articles to which I referred. He further stated that the denomination firmly dissociated themselves from the work of the Unification Church.

I discussed this response with a Welsh colleague, who offered to accompany me to their morning service one Sunday, since their worship might be in the Welsh language rather than English. As it turned out, the service was entirely in English, apart from some occurrences of glossolalia, and I also had the good fortune to be told that my previous correspondent was not present on that occasion. Having effectively been given a clean slate, I decided not to mention the Unification Church specifically, but to say that I was interested in their denomination's missionary work in East Asia. This disclosure elicited a quite different response, and was met with some enthusiasm: 'That would be Pastor Joshua McCabe', I was told, and I was given his address for further correspondence. I followed up this disclosure by writing to Pastor McCabe, again mentioning East Asia rather than the Unification Church, and received a very detailed response in which he volunteered information about his encounters with Sun Myung Moon, and painted a very different – and extremely negative – picture from the one recounted by the Unification Church. We had a friendly exchange of correspondence, which ended with his hope that 'Brother Chryssides' would meet him in the air at Christ's second coming! (1 Thessalonians 4:17).

Did I do the right thing? The alternative would have been not to follow up this incident, resulting in incomplete research on the Unification Movement. However, although my approach to the Pentecostal congregation may have lacked complete transparency, McCabe was eighty-five years old at the time he wrote to me, and his testimony would have been lost forever. A substantial amount of the material on the Unification Church's early years is probably hagiography rather than history, and it was therefore useful to have a counterbalancing external source of information. The Family Federation for World Peace and Unification (FFWPU, as the main institution is now called) continues to publish its own version of the story of McCabe's visit, which is one-sided, to say the least. I am glad to have had the opportunity to publish the other side of the story, complete with McCabe's correspondence in full (Chryssides 2017: 85–100; Family Federation 2017). In any case, one might ask what full disclosure really amounts to, since it is not possible to mention every aspect of one's research. I did not lie to anyone but if I had been probed further, I would have felt obliged to mention the Unification Church.

My second ethical dilemma involved confidentiality. By confidentiality we normally imply name-anonymity, since the very fact that we publish our work entails that much of the information we gain from fieldwork is not confidential. Confidentiality is usually associated with information collected during field-work, but there are other forms of confidential material, such as those belonging to a religious organisation, which they do not want to fall into the wrong hands. One such confidential document, belonging to the Watch Tower Society, is an elders' manual entitled '*Shepherd the Flock of God*', first published in 2010, and subsequently revised at various stages. The manual, whose title is a quotation from 1 Peter 5:2 (hence the inverted commas), defines in detail how their office-bearers are appointed and 'deleted' (removed from office); how to counsel members of the congregation; which offences merit judicial action; and how congregational discipline should be exercised. One might have thought that, in the interests of transparency, and to clarify the organisation's expectations of members' behaviour, such a document would be made available to everyone. However, the Watch Tower Society has taken a different view, and stipulates that only active elders should possess a copy. The front matter reads:

> A copy is issued to each appointed elder. If an elder is deleted for reasons other than moving to another congregation with a favorable recommendation, he should turn over this handbook to the Congregation Service Committee. (Watch Tower 2020: introduction)

Since I was writing at the time about Jehovah's Witnesses' disciplinary proce-dures, this was an important volume to consult, and numerous other writers on the Watch Tower Society obviously possessed copies, since they cited the publication. The situation was further complicated by the fact that many such documents can be found on the Internet. It is rumoured that such material has been put in the public domain by disenchanted members who do not wish to leave the organisation but who are prepared to leak such information, so it was not difficult to locate and download the document. Wanting to maintain good relationships with the Society's office-bearers, I thought the best course of action was to ask staff at the Society's international headquarters in New York if they might be prepared, exceptionally, to send me a copy, but they declined. This created an awkward situation: the Society did not want me to have access to the document, yet I already had one in my possession. On the one hand, researchers are normally expected to maintain confidentiality; on the other hand, failure to discuss its contents would have resulted in a serious gap in my research, and I might justly have been criticised for not mentioning the organisation's ways of dealing with judicial matters. After some deliberation, I decided that '*Shepherd the Flock of God*' was already in the public domain, even if this was against the wishes of the Watch Tower organisation, and that I would use it, since it was important for my study. Despite my fear that my action would damage important relationships that I had built up over the years, fortunately I incurred no criticism from Jehovah's Witnesses for using the work.

My decision in a third situation was probably more contentious. Some years ago a prominent exponent of prosperity theology was scheduled to speak at a meeting in my area. Prosperity theology – sometimes also called the 'prosperity gospel', the Word of Faith Movement or 'seed faith' – is a doctrine that gained momentum in the 1950s among certain Protestant fundamentalists. They claim that God wants followers to be materially wealthy, and this can be achieved by planting 'seeds' in the form of monetary offerings to the organisation. The movement is sometimes encapsulated in the maxim 'Name it and claim it!', meaning that the believer can identify a material benefit and obtain it by 'planting seeds', typically in the form of prayer and financial donations. The attendees did not appear to be particularly wealthy, and this was confirmed by the meeting's theme, which was largely about how to get out of debt. At one point the audience was asked to chant in unison, 'I want to be – debt free!' The guest speaker was not in debt, and in fact openly acknowledged that he was very wealthy: this was evidently what God wanted, and he attributed his success to following his own teachings on financial matters. The speaker offered various books and paraphernalia for sale, and an incentive was that each month two supporters were selected randomly to have all their debts paid off. Towards the end of the meeting, financial contributions were sought. However, this was not in the more usual form of passing around a collection plate; instead, attendees were issued with blank slips of paper on which they were asked to write their names and their credit card details.

How does one extricate oneself from such a situation? Several options were possible. One was compliance, but divulging one's financial details is usually inadvisable, and in any case I thought it was inappropriate to support the organisation and put even more wealth into its coffers. Another option would have been to leave the meeting at that junction, but I wanted to witness it right to the end. Alternatively, I could write a message on my paper, expressing my disapproval of the event, but that would have been embarrassing, and a researcher usually endeavours to observe rather than disrupt or criticise. I have to confess that I employed the most obvious extricating tactic – writing a false name and a random sixteen-digit number. Of course, my action militated against the usual expectations of honesty and avoidance of deception, but the situation seemed to be a clear example of financial and spiritual abuse of a disadvantaged and somewhat naive group of people.

Conclusion

The comedian Groucho Marx once said, 'Those are my principles, and if you don't like them . . . well, I have others'. There is a serious point here, however. Statements such as the Concordat, and the preambles to various professional codes of practice set out a list of virtues, such as 'honesty, rigour, transparency, and respect' (British Association 2019). Virtue ethics has a long history, going back as far as Plato and Aristotle, but there are other ethical systems. One common criticism of virtue ethics is that it tells us what to *be,* not what to *do.* I like to think that I am honest, but what is the honest course of action when I am asked to donate to a religious leader whom I believe to be dishonest? Research should certainly be rigorous, but what if rigour involves lack of transparency about my purposes, in the interests of acquiring important information? Who merits respect at a prosperity gospel meeting – the wealthy, exploitative preacher, or the less wealthy and possibly gullible congregation? There are other ethical systems that focus on *doing* rather than *being.* A utilitarian approach would consider the degree of human welfare that would benefit from the various courses of action that are open to the researcher. Other ethical theories are based on human rights, and an ethical dilemma could be approached from a human rights angle. For example, does the availability of confidential material in the public domain give me the right to access and disclose its contents, or has an organisation the right to determine who is entitled to read it? Again, respect for persons, a fundamental principle in Immanuel Kant's ethical theory, emphasises the importance of the integrity and autonomy of individuals, and was one of three key elements in the Belmont Report (DHEW 1978) on biomedical and behavioural research, the other two principles being beneficence and justice.

It is evident that there are no clear solutions for conducting ethical fieldwork. My argument in this section has suggested that there is an important distinction between biomedical research and research in the social sciences, including the study of NRMs. Unfortunately, many academic researchers are constrained by heavy-handed research committees that seek to impose rigid rules and regulations in the name of ethics. Clearly researchers must seek the approval of their institution, where needed, and abide by its requirements, but in the field of NRMs we will continue to encounter situations that require our personal ethical judgement, and cannot always be resolved by appealing to formal codes of practice.

6 Online Fieldwork

The advent of the Internet has changed the nature of fieldwork, and indeed the study of religion more widely. The Internet is still a recent innovation, and continues to develop. 1 January 1983 is regarded as the date of the Internet's inception (University of Georgia n.d.), but it only achieved widespread use in the late 1990s. When the Heaven's Gate suicides hit the headlines in 1997, the news that its members had been running a company called Higher Source, which created websites, was met with some amazement, since the nature of the Internet was not widely understood. Douglas Cowan reports that one commentator announced:

> We talked to some cult experts last night, and what we found – this is going to shock you – some 10,000 cult sites on the World Wide Web. Literally every cult, large to small, has staked out some sort of a space in cyberspace. (Gina Smith, *Good Morning America*, 1997; cited in Chryssides 2011: 139)

and another explained:

> 'Web pages are viewable using software called a "browser,"' and readers 'can see information displayed in magazine-style "pages,"' some of which 'have sounds and even snippets of video or animation'. (Miller 1997; cited in Chryssides 2011: 139)

Twenty-five years on, such statements are laughable. It would be surprising if there were now only 10,000 websites relating to NRMs, and only a few people now need any explanation of what browsers and webpages are. Looking back on these reports on Heaven's Gate serves to demonstrate just how far technology, and particularly the Internet, have progressed in such a relatively short time. As online religion has developed and become increasingly sophisticated, Internet studies have progressed correspondingly. Those of us who used the Internet in its early years will recall that information was transferred through telephone cables, often resulting in slow transmission, particularly if visuals – especially motion pictures – were involved. The invention of Wi-Fi in 1997 and progressive increases in bandwidth resulted in considerable improvements. Skype made its appearance in 2003, and social media began a year later, with the introduction of 'The Facebook', at first confined to student use, in 2004. (The word 'the' was dropped later.) YouTube commenced in 2005, followed by Twitter in 2006 (Craig 2022). All this enabled much more interactive use of the Internet, as bulletin boards, chat rooms, blogs, and electronic discussion lists became commonplace. These developments gave rise to the formation of online communities and at this stage the Internet developed into a new type of space – cyberspace. The Internet was no longer an electronically accessible library, but a network of communities in which the scholar could undertake fieldwork.

Morten T. Højsgaard and Margit Warburg suggested a number of stages or 'waves' of studies of religion online, corresponding to developments in online religion. The first stage was the early days of Internet use by religious organisations, where the principal use was disseminating information. This was essentially information about the principal beliefs and practices of the religious organisation, with details about timings of activities. A few individuals created their own webpages, commenting on their own forms of spirituality. Corresponding with these early attempts at online innovation, research on the role of the Internet in religion tended to be descriptive, accompanied by speculations about the Internet's future capabilities and utopian expectations about its possibilities. The second wave was more nuanced, emphasising people rather than technology, and noting the different ways in which religious practitioners operated within the possibilities afforded by online religion. The difference is sometimes characterised by distinguishing 'religion online' from 'online religion'. (The former principally involves the dissemination of information about religion, while the latter involves participative online practice.) Højsgaard and Warburg were writing in 2005, and envisaged a third wave developing in the future, in which novel forms of religion, and indeed new religions, might develop, thus requiring a 'bricolage of scholarship', in which scholars with different disciplinary backgrounds might collaborate in order to understand these new forms. (Højsgaard and Warburg 2005: 1–9).

One main advantage that the Internet offers to NRMs is that they now have a publicly accessible voice. Since most of them now have their own websites, in which they can disseminate their beliefs and practices, unfiltered by adverse criticism by their detractors, the public need no longer to rely on the countercult literature that is regularly found in Christian bookstores, and which in the past was the most accessible source of information to the general reader. The Internet, of course, enables more than the dissemination of information, and researchers are now not only able to check their data against their experiences in fieldwork, but can actually view rituals, ceremonies, services of worship, interviews with leaders and with their commentators – all of which would have had limited availability to researchers if they had had to trek around such events in traditional ways in physical space.

Some NRMs exist principally online. The originators of 'invented religions' (see Section 1) do not claim to base their ideas on factual truth, but have either offered them as parody, or else have developed forms of spirituality from science fiction. The best-known examples are the Church of the Flying Spaghetti Monster, Discordianism, the Church of the SubGenius, and Jediism.

Although such organisations originated on the Internet, members occasionally organise in-person meetings; however, they are most readily accessed by researchers online.

Creating Online Versions of Religion

Even before the Covid pandemic caused worshippers to adapt their activities to online versions, various attempts at online worship had already commenced. One early attempt was the Church of Fools, sponsored by the Methodist Church in the United Kingdom in 2004. (The name is an allusion to Saint Paul's statement that believers should be 'fools for Christ', alluding to 1 Corinthians 4:10.) By present standards, the attempt was fairly crude. Worshippers appropriated an avatar, and could move around a rudimentary church in cyberspace and attend services of worship at set times by occupying a pew. Because of limited bandwidth, attendees were restricted to 25 participants, and any additional attendees could simply lurk as 'ghosts', having observer rather than participant–observer status. Participation, however, was confined to typing the words of the hymns, in so far as one could keep up with the pace of the pre-recorded singing, and typing 'Amen' at the end of prayers. The project was abandoned after only a few months because of lack of funding. Attendees took their worship seriously, regarding this section of cyberspace as sacred space, and anyone who displayed an irreverent attitude – for example making their avatar bow before the coffee machine – could be evicted.

The notion of how or whether parts of cyberspace can be sacred space has been an issue. One solution was to link cyberspace activity with its counterpart in physical space. The London Internet Church offered its visitors the facility to 'light' candles online, with the assurance that this activity would be matched by an office-bearer in St Stephen Walbrook lighting a physical candle and offering intercessions on the supplicant's behalf. Candles are not inherently sacred, and prayer can be undertaken without physical substance, but more problematic were the Christian sacraments, in which physical bread and wine are consumed, and physical water is used to baptise infants and catechumens. One attempt to solve the problem was 'Bishop' Jonathan Blake's Open Episcopal Church, set up in 2016, which offers a Post the Host service. Potential worshippers are invited to send Blake an email giving their contact details, whereupon Blake, an ordained priest in the Episcopal tradition, is empowered to consecrate communion wafers which he will send by post. The worshipper can then view a selection of YouTube versions of the Mass, over which Blake presides, and consume the Eucharistic elements at the appropriate time during the service. Needless to say, Post the Host is controversial, since the bread and wine of holy communion should be treated with due respect, and not be handled by postal workers, or consumed without a priest's direct supervision.

More ambitious is 'Bishop' D. J. Soto's VR Church, which the congregation attends by donning headsets, and adopting an avatar which enables them not only to listen to the service, but to move around the cyber-congregation and interact with other members using quasi-tactile activities, such as standing and sitting, shaking hands, even hugging. The VR Church allows cyber-baptism; although one cannot use real water in cyberspace, the sound of flowing water can be simulated, and other aspects of the rite can be conducted. Christians may debate whether this is a valid baptism, but those who have undergone Soto's cyber-baptism claim to have found it a moving experience.

Online religion is not, of course, confined to acts of worship. As the Internet has developed, there are facilities for online pilgrimage, and there are various online games and activities, ranging from quizzes to higher tech creations such as strategy games related to religious themes. One Jehovah's Witness has (unofficially) devised a game in which the player helps to create Jehovah's everlasting paradise on earth – a project that requires human effort as well as divine encouragement. Possibly better-known are the strategy games devised as follow-ups to the bestselling *Left Behind* novels by Tim LaHaye and Jerry B. Jenkins, in which players assume roles in their end-time fiction.[2] Those engaging in online fieldwork are certainly not short of subject matter.

The Covid-19 Pandemic

The Covid-19 pandemic caused a significant change in online religious activity, affecting not only NRMs themselves, but the methods of researching them. Faced with lockdown, the majority of religious communities undertook to act responsibly, and avoided meeting in physical space, as they had been accustomed. Most of their activities went online, and many who had not been familiar with online activity swiftly learned how to use the relevant technology and participate remotely (See Chryssides and Cohn-Sherbok 2023).

One of the interesting features of online fieldwork was to monitor how religious organisations adapted to online worship. Some were already well down the route to placing their material online. Jehovah's Witnesses, for example, had long since ensured that much online material was already available, in the form of Watch Tower publications, videos, music, interviews with Governing Body members, a news desk, and much more. When they adopted the practice of writing letters to householders instead of house-to-house

---

[2] Tim LaHaye and Jerry Jenkins (1995–2007), *Left Behind*, 16 volumes (Carol Stream, IL: Tyndale House). Five film adaptations have been made as of this writing.

evangelising, I always sent a response, which on one occasion led to a Zoom meeting with the author, and later a house call from another two publishers – the Society's name for their evangelists – once their house-to-house evangelism was permissible again.

In the United Kingdom, as in numerous other countries, the 2020 lockdown occurred a short time before the Witnesses' annual Memorial service, which is the only festival celebrated in their calendar. This service involves the use of the physical substances of unleavened bread and red wine, and therefore it was interesting to see how they would deal with a ritual that could not readily be performed without physical materials. Since Jehovah's Witnesses do not believe that any supernatural miracle takes place during the rite, they saw no problem in inviting online attendees to have their own bread and wine ready to hand at their computer screens. They directed would-be participants to a video, which demonstrated how unleavened bread could be prepared: although it does not involve any special consecration, there are rules governing the recipe for these emblems, as they call them. Mainstream Christian congregations encountered less surmountable problems, since it is generally held that bread and wine cannot be consecrated at a distance, and many want to ensure that the symbols of Christ's body and blood are duly safeguarded by being consumed during the service or disposed of in an acceptable way afterwards. Apart from having to prepare the emblems appropriately, attending the Memorial online was much easier than attending it in person. I had invitations from three different congregations, and was able to choose which one to attend. Attendees were still expected to observe the appropriate dress code – suits and ties for men, skirts below the knees for women – since an over-casual attitude to the Memorial is discouraged.

Jehovah's Witnesses perceived an advantage in meeting online, which they subsequently made a point of implementing for all meetings, not merely the Memorial. This enabled the sick and the housebound to be part of the gathering, on the same terms as everyone else; previously the practice was to set up a telephone link so that absent members could hear the service, although not see it. The added visual component was a definite advantage, and after the ending of the lockdown, Jehovah's Witnesses, like numerous other denominations, now worship in hybrid mode, which is much more inclusive. Since some of their meetings are interactive, enabling attendees to make comments at certain points, those at home became familiar with the practice of raising electronic hands, and the service conductor makes a point of looking out for these, as well as for physical hands within the Kingdom Hall. One aspect of worship that does not currently lend itself to online activity is congregational singing: because of differences in time lags in different attendees' equipment, attempts at communal singing result in a cacophony. However, as technology advances, this may cease to be a problem in the future.

Most readers will probably have experienced that their online fieldwork has been combined with online gatherings with other scholars. As well as being more convenient to attend and less expensive to organise, online seminars and conferences can readily become international rather than national events, since attendees are not bound by physical constraints or expense, but only by differences in their time zones.

The Boundaries of Fieldwork

All this raises the question of the extent to which the use of online technologies constitutes fieldwork. Can fieldwork be an activity that is undertaken from one's desk, or must there be physical interaction between the researcher and the communities that are being studied? The Internet in fact has added a new dimension to the concept of community. Communities can now consist of people living remotely from each other, but who meet in cyberspace. The community of scholars has broadened to facilitate much greater international collaboration; religious communities are no longer defined by their locality; and discussion forums have created communities, both of religious adherents and of researchers who can be drawn from a wide variety of international locations.

Online ethnography can therefore be regarded as an adaptation of traditional ethnography to communities on the Internet, which are created through cyberspace. This is sometimes also called virtual ethnography, netography, or cyberethnography. Online research into NRMs is wider than ethnography: accessing NRMs' websites, in which there is no human interaction is effectively akin to consulting a vast library, while watching video material, such as YouTube, can be compared with employing modern technological facilities in conventional libraries. Nonetheless, both of these are invaluable to researchers, and YouTube channels can involve interaction between individuals through comment boxes, and bear some resemblance to electronic discussion groups.

Of course, there are limitations on undertaking online fieldwork. Viewing a ritual on one's screen makes the researcher reliant on what the organisation has selected. The researcher is denied the opportunity to decide the aspects on which to focus, or to look around to gauge the composition and reactions of the congregation. But notwithstanding these limitations, the opportunities afforded by the Internet considerably outweigh such disadvantages. There are obvious benefits, such as being able to download, replay, check the veracity of what one has heard and seen, and reference the material.

As Oliver Krüger (2005) points out, problems with any empirical research involve issues of validity and reliability, but such problems are intensified in online research. If I am researching Wicca online, for example, how do I decide on which online communities to focus? A straightforward Google search yields 23,900,000 webpages, although not all of these are online communities by any means. Krüger notes that different search engines may prioritise differently, and only locate URLs in the surface web, leaving out the deep web, which is normally only accessible with specialised search facilities. To what extent this is a major problem, of course, might well be debated; after all, similar problems exist in physical space, where I may be unaware of existing Wiccan groups, may not be able to access communities that meet in private, and can only undertake fieldwork on no more than a handful.

What I might do, as Krüger suggests, is to rely on referrals by other researchers, or else simply adopt a case-study approach, focusing on one or perhaps a small selection of online communities. Problems of validity and reliability would then only arise if I were to suggest that such groups were representative of Wicca more widely, or if I assumed that other communities outside my sphere of investigation behaved in a similar way. Krüger also points out that online material can swiftly be removed, and that group moderators have the power to censor members' input. We only become acquainted with those who are vocal within a group, not those who simply lurk. Further, it is difficult to associate online identities with physical characteristics, since the web allows anonymity, allowing users to hide behind screen names, enabling them to assume new identities and to conceal characteristics that they do not wish to reveal. It is not possible to tell whether the pseudonymous 'Enlightened Ermintrude' is male or female, young or old, white or Black, disabled or able-bodied, thus making it impossible to comment on the group's demographic composition, as is possible in physical space. Internet users can provide 'About' information, but many prefer not to divulge personal details, or may invent fictitious profiles.

The use of screen names raises questions about anonymity and confidentiality. Is it legitimate to cite someone's screen name when writing about one's online research, and is it legitimate to use one's own screen name when researching, without divulging one's true off-line identity? On the one hand, as Krüger suggests, a screen name might be regarded as a new form of anonymity, while on the other hand, the BASR Ethical Guidelines (2019) regard a screen name as a new identity that its owner has created, which assumes a life of its own, and has its own rights of privacy and confidentiality, just as someone would wish their identity to be respected if they change their offline name. There are currently no clear answers to this question, although certainly if one's offline identity could be inferred from its online material, the researcher would be obliged to observe the normal conventions of name anonymity. When researchers only use a screen name, without indicating their true identity or purpose, the research becomes covert, and one would need to consider whether such covert online research is necessary.

Problems in Online Fieldwork

Various scholars have identified problems in online research. In his chapter entitled 'The Internet', Douglas E. Cowan (2011: 459–73) finds three broad issues. First there are problems of ephemerality and durability of online information. On the one hand, valuable material can disappear from the Internet without trace: a moderator can delete comments in a chat room, or entire websites can vanish if the owner of the domain name does not renew a subscription. Although some material is retrievable through the Wayback Machine,[3] retention of data relies on a web user having made an image of the relevant pages. Conversely, obsolete online material might continue to appear when a webmaster fails to update webpages. Although one can recognise out-of-date material if its author has put a date on a website, many webpages are undated, and hence it is important to triangulate online material with other sources of data.

A second problem relates to identity and authority. While the Internet can be said to be a leveller, since one can assume an identity which avoids discrimination on the grounds of race, gender, disability, and other human characteristics, it can also place experts and well-intentioned amateurs on the same footing. Often the credentials of a web author are unverifiable, and hence, as Cowan points out, we cannot know whether someone is a genuine high priestess, or whether a webmaster has the level of academic expertise one would expect from a website purporting to be authoritative. Cowan cites the example of the Apologetics Index (www.apologeticsindex.org), which purports to give authoritative information about NRMs (and indeed contains some useful material), but whose author does not display any academic credentials in religion.

A third, and more difficult, issue is ethics. Academics are accustomed to two key principles of research involving human subjects: disclosure and informed consent. However, in the context of online research the issue of informed consent is much less clear. If I am on an e-list or on social media, to what extent are the other users consenting to my presence? One could argue, of course, that

---

[3] The Wayback Machine, managed by the nonprofit organisation Internet Archive, is a digital archive of websites posted on the World Wide Web. It captures snapshots in time of virtually all websites, making them available even when they have gone offline. See https://www.archive.org.

moderators can make the list closed if they do not want outside visitors, but I may not know how to contact the author, particularly if he or she has adopted a screen name, and I may decide to use a contribution because it displays characteristics such as religious hatred or prejudice, in which case the contributor would probably decline to give permission. If we insisted on informant consent, this could prevent certain viewpoints from being discussed in one's writing, and would effectively give contributors the power of censorship. Informed consent might well militate against academic freedom and the reader's right to know. In general, one key issue, on which the jury is still out, is whether the Internet is like a gigantic library, from which one is entitled to borrow and use its material, or whether at least part of it is more like conversations between individuals, on whom the online researcher is at times an eavesdropper rather than an accepted discussant.

Online Surveys

The Internet affords the opportunity for researchers to undertake online survey work. Setting up facilities for data collection can be easy, but it also has serious pitfalls. In 2019 some researchers in the University of Utrecht were allowed to set up some pages within the institution's website to enable victims of sexual abuse among Jehovah's Witnesses to recount their experiences. Although the researchers stated that responses could be positive as well as negative, it was inevitable that the vast majority of respondents recounted negative ones. Advertising for respondents, of course, can give a piece of research an obvious bias; the majority of Kingdom Hall attendees, who have not experienced any sexual impropriety, are unlikely to respond to an invitation of this kind. How many of us respond to all of the many surveys that come our way on the Internet? Many commercial organisations now use means of identifying fake reviews, but there appeared to be no safeguards against respondents completing the Utrecht survey multiple times, and it is doubtful whether the researchers made obvious checks on whether multiple responses came from the same IP address. The researchers obtained 751 responses, which superficially might suggest that a high level of sexual abuse takes place within the Watch Tower organisation. However, of the 422 that provided accounts of sexual abuse, 214 reported personal experiences, while 208 gave information on behalf of someone else, 84 per cent of which were of multiple incidents. Roughly half the cases were among family members, compared with approximately one quarter by fellow members, and 4 per cent by office-bearers. Interpreting the data was also impeded by overlapping categories: for example, some victims may have had multiple predators, and some predators multiple victims, and some who reported personal experience of sexual abuse may have found that others reported the same instances on their behalf. Most of the reports were of incidents between 2007 and 2019, and this too requires some interpretation. Might it indicate that instances have declined in recent years, or might it be the case that, since victims might tend to be young, they have not yet reached an age at which they would be able to report them?

This investigation was not simply botched research by inexperienced students. It was commissioned by CIAOSN (Centre d'information et d'avis sur les organisations sectaires nuisibles, Centre for Information and Advice on Harmful Sectarian Organisations), a governmental cult-monitoring organisation. A Belgian newspaper reporter subsequently picked up on the report, published an article which led to litigation, which finally went to the Court of Brussels in 2022. The court found in favour of the Jehovah's Witnesses, criticising the methodology of the report's (anonymous) authors, and noting, inter alia, that no Jehovah's Witnesses had been consulted in its compilation (Folk 2021; Introvigne 2022b; Utrecht University 2020).

Ex-members Online

A further feature of online religion is that it has facilitated the creation of ex-member groups. Formerly countercult and anticult opposition to NRMs occurred through the creation of physically based organisations, such as the American Family Foundation (now the International Cultic Studies Association) in the United States, and Family Action Information and Rescue (FAIR) and the Reachout Trust in the United Kingdom. These and other such organisations have used traditional methods of circulating newsletters, producing pamphlets, and organising in-person seminars. A small handful of groups were cult-specific, such as CONCERN in the United Kingdom (focusing on the Children of God), but these tended to be short-lived, or else developed into more general organisations that challenged NRMs more widely. The greater accessibility afforded by the Internet, combined with its international nature has facilitated online groups that focus on specific NRMs.

A number of researchers have taken recourse to using ex-member websites as sources from which to select informants. In two doctoral theses which I recently viewed, the candidates contacted members from ex-member Facebook lists, and asked them to recommend others as a snowball sample. Unlike the Utrecht University researchers, at least they followed up online contact with in-person interviews. Typically the sample was small, which is understandable given the timescale in which such research must be completed, and the number ranged from eight to twelve participants. They were asked about their experiences of membership and of leaving the organisation; the interviews were then transcribed and coded on various themes, and predictably the comments were negative. These researchers identify their work as 'interpretative phenomenological analysis', and justify the small sample on the grounds of saturation of information. Obviously, if one draws one's sample from the same pool of like-minded participants, the researcher is likely to experience information saturation very quickly. If it is pointed out that the participants may not be typical of ex-members more widely, the researcher can respond that the findings cannot necessarily be extrapolated to ex-members in general, but it is a survey of how these particular participants responded. When it is mentioned that some of their information is incorrect – for example, one participant referred to a *Watchtower* article which did not exist – it can be replied that such a survey does not purport to show what is necessarily true about the Watch Tower organisation, but rather how the participants see their experiences in hindsight.

Although it can be acknowledged that every piece of research has its scope and limitations, such studies are misleading, since they focus unduly on the disaffected ex-member. Their proliferation creates an imbalance of research in the field, possibly suggesting that these attitudes are typical of those who leave a controversial organisation. It is also difficult to see the value of such studies: what does one expect to hear from those who belong to an ex-member group, and refer their own contacts to the researcher? Some samples can be only too convenient to locate, and such research raises the issue of whether research is worthwhile when the outcome is thoroughly predictable.

The anonymity afforded by the Internet also gives a voice to those who belong to an organisation and have reservations which they cannot express openly. It enables a degree of 'coming out', allowing a dissenting opinion to be aired, but without identifying the author. One such example is the Association of Jehovah's Witnesses for the Reform of Blood (AJWRB); these claim to be elders who disagree with the Society's stance prohibiting blood transfusion. Within the organisation, anyone who openly expresses dissent runs the risk of judicial action, and in the case of such a fundamental policy, these elders would certainly be disfellowshipped, one consequence of which would be shunning by their fellow members. There are said to be other Jehovah's Witnesses, some of whom are congregational elders, who have serious doubts about other matters, but feel that they cannot afford to lose family and friends. They prefer to give the appearance of being faithful members, rather than face the consequences of disfellowshipping.

Conclusion

The advent of the Internet has given rise to enormous changes, both in the way in which scholars research their material, and in the religions themselves. Even many of the Amish now avail themselves of information technology, despite their historic refusal to adopt secular values and mechanised forms of transport. The continued development of the Internet demonstrates the necessity for longitudinal study of the various NRMs, and indeed traditional, religions. The Internet will continue to provide us both with the subject matter and the tools of research for decades to come.

7 Epilogue

New religions change. Some become defunct, new ones arise, some split into schisms, and most of them age. Much has changed since the 1960s and 1970s, as founder–leaders have died, and inevitable problems of succession have resulted. Members have grown older, and second- and third-generation members have now appeared, raising issues about parenting, education, and faith maintenance. Technology has moved on, and the recent Covid-19 pandemic has brought about significant changes in the ways in which NRMs operate. Public interest has changed too. Although brainwashing remains a popular presumption, other issues have emerged, such as sexual abuse, and religious (or quasi-religious) movements that appear to be linked with terrorist activities or far-right politics. All this demonstrates the continued need for fieldwork to keep pace with these changes.

The public interest in the NRMs that came into prominence in the 1960s and 1970s, and which was followed by academic study, has somewhat eclipsed the 'old new' religions. Mormonism has had its scholars for some considerable time, and is well covered in the literature, and interest in Jehovah's Witnesses is now emerging as an area of scholarly investigation. However, there remains a dearth of literature on Christadelphianism, Spiritualism, Theosophy, and British Israelism, among others.

There are also several themes that remain under-researched. Although the majority of founder–leaders of the 1960s and 1970s NRMs have now died, a large sector of the anticult movement continues to propagate the view that naive young seekers become brainwashed or hypnotised by the messianic leader. By contrast, NRM scholars have given considerable discussion to changes that the leader's death has necessitated, the various ways in which conversion occurs, and how problems of succession are resolved.

The issue of death rituals also deserves examination, and offers scope for further fieldwork. Followers of Hindu and Buddhist-related NRMs cannot conduct funerals in the traditional manner of their parent religions. This is partly because it would be illegal in the West to burn funeral pyres to dispose of bodies, and partly because it would probably cause deep offence to the more conventional friends and relatives of the deceased. One member of the Western Buddhist Order (now Triratna) told me some years ago that one of their deceased members was simply given a conventional Western-style Christian funeral, since this is what his family would prefer, not being members of the Order. However, his ashes were placed in a stupa in one of their shrine rooms. Attitudes of families and friends, however, may well have changed as a result of the decline in Christian allegiance over the past half-century. As members themselves age, NRMs increasingly face the question of how they deal with death more widely. NRM research has acknowledged the presence of second- and third-generation members and reflected this in the literature, but there remains relatively little work on rites of passage, such as how NRMs deal with death and other life rituals.

A further gap in scholarship relates to ex-members and marginal members. It tends to be assumed that the NRM convert is one who joins with conviction and has an excess of enthusiasm for the organisation, and it is inevitable that the fieldworker tends to encounter the members who are most in evidence and who are keen to relate their experiences. However, the participant–observer can only observe those who are present, not those who are absent and who may be less enthusiastic. As Stephen Gregg and I have pointed out, there are all kinds of insider and outsider in religious organisations, ranging from those who form the inner circle of policymaking to those who are simply on a mailing list. It is not easy to access the occasional attendee, the apathetic member, or those who are wavering about whether to join or whether to leave. If the problem of access could be overcome, some extremely interesting data could be revealed about what may be the more typical adherents to NRMs. Likewise, the ex-members who are regularly encountered are the vociferous ones, but we have good reason to believe that they are not at all typical of the average leaver. While the vociferous ex-members can be readily found by accessing ex-member and anticult groups, the silent majority, as we have called them, are difficult to locate (Gregg and Chryssides 2017: 20–32).

Much of the fieldwork to date on new religions has focused on the worldviews – what they believe, what texts they recognise as authoritative, what their exponents tell us in interviews and through questionnaires – and participant–observation has involved noting features of rituals and ceremonies. However, there are other aspects of NRMs that are gradually gaining recognition in the study of new religions. Sound and sight are by no means the only aspects of religion. Graham Harvey has edited a series on Religion and the Senses, and though it does not exclusively focus on new religious movements, it highlights the fact that religion involves food and food sharing, music, artefacts, and costume. A number of scholars in Australia have done recent work on what they call cultural production, focusing on religious architecture, music, dance, and territorial issues. All these are topics that could profitably be taken into the arena of NRM fieldwork. The topic of religion in museums has received some coverage, again in connection with traditional religions. While it might appear that NRMs are too new to feature in museums, the demise of some founder–leaders has led to the creation of exhibitions of memorabilia. One example is the museum at Cheongpyeong in South Korea, which features artefacts that belonged to Sun Myung Moon, and aroused comment for featuring a Snickers bar wrapper and Coca-Cola can belonging to Moon, which are regarded as akin to secondary relics (Straits Times 2016). There are numerous exhibitions in Los Angeles relating to the work of L. Ron Hubbard, as well as the Hubbard busts that one finds in every Scientology org. One might also add the exhibitions recounting Mormon history in Salt Lake City, as well as one by Unarians in San Diego. Interesting work could be undertaken assessing their origins and function, and how they relate to the subsequent practice by these faiths.

There remains an issue about the areas of academia that might be stake-holders in the study of NRMs. As is evident from Section 2 on landmarks in NRM studies, the prerogative for studying NRMs has tended to reside with sociologists. Without wishing to deny the importance of sociological study, any single disciplinary approach is bound to be limited, and by focusing on the societal implications of new religions, sociologists have frequently paid scant attention to the worldviews of the NRMs under study. One glaring example is the treatment of prophecy, which numerous sociologists, taking their cue from Festinger, have invariably assumed to be prediction (typically of the world's end), and which is doomed to failure. These assumptions differ markedly from scholars who are more familiar with biblical studies, and are more likely to regard the prophet as delivering a timely and successful message from God. However, the blame for any deficiencies in understanding should not rest exclusively with sociologists; those who have designed the curriculum in Divinity faculties continue to shun new religions, deeming them to be unworthy of study. A more interdisciplinary approach to NRM studies, in my view, would prove to be extremely fruitful.

Finally, as every NRM scholar will agree, fieldwork takes time, and the process between commencing one's research and final publication can take years. This contrasts with journalism, where editors expect instant copy when some newsworthy event occurs. The anticult movement is only too ready to provide knee-jerk reactions, telling the media that a group is a 'typical cult' and that its members are brainwashed. Unfortunately, public opinion tends to be shaped by the view that is presented first, and which social psychologists call the primacy effect. Once a popular belief becomes implanted, it is difficult to dislodge. This means that academic study wages a losing battle against misinformation. How we reverse this trend and encourage the public to be patient for reliable information remains a challenge in which fieldworkers will be engaged for years to come.

Abbreviations

AAR	American Academy of Religion
AJWRB	Association of Jehovah's Witnesses for the Reform of Blood
AUDTRS	Association of University Departments of Theology and Religious Studies
BASR	British Association for the Study of Religions
CIAOSN	Centre d'information et d'avis sur les organisations sectaires nuisibles [Centre for Information and Advice on Harmful Sectarian Organisations]
DHEW	Department of Health, Education, and Welfare
FAIR	Family Action Information and Rescue
FFWPU	Family Federation for World Peace and Unification
IP	Internet Provider
ISKCON	International Society for Krishna Consciousness
LGBTQ	Lesbian, Gay, Bisexual, Transgender, and Queer
MO	Moses David (David Berg)
NRM	New Religious Movement
OT	Operating Thetan
PIMO	Physically In, Mentally Out
SDA	Seventh-day Adventist
SGI	Soka Gakkai International
UC	Unification Church
UFO	Unidentified Flying Object
VR	Virtual Reality

References

Adherents.com (2019). Unification Church. https://web.archive.org/web/20170611093832/http:/www.adherents.com/Na/Na_638.html. Accessed 16 May 2023.

American Academy of Religion (2016). Responsible Research Practices: A Statement on Standards of Professional Conduct for AAR Members. www.aarweb.org/AARMBR/About-AAR-/Board-of-Directors-/Board-Resolutions-/Responsible-Research-Practices.aspx. Accessed 17 May 2023.

American Anthropological Association (1998). Code of Ethics of the American Anthropological Association. www.americananthro.org/ParticipateAnd Advocate/Content.aspx?ItemNumber=1656. Accessed 2 June 2023.

American Sociological Association (2023). A History of the ASA Code of Ethics. www.asanet.org/a-history-of-the-asa-code-of-ethics/. Accessed 2 June 2023.

Aristotle (1934). *Nicomachean Ethics*. transl. Rackham. Aristotle in 23 Volumes, Vol. 19, translated by H. Rackham. Cambridge, MA: Harvard University Press.

Arweck, E. and M. D. Stringer (2002). *Theorizing Faith: The Insider/Outsider Problem in the Study of Ritual*. Birmingham: University of Birmingham Press.

Balch, R. W. and D. Taylor (1977). Seekers and Saucers: The Role of the Cultic Milieu in Joining a UFO. *The American Behavioral Scientist* 20 (6): 839–60.

Barker, E. (1984). *The Making of a Moonie: Choice or Brainwashing?* Oxford: Blackwell.

Barker, E. (1989). *New Religious Movements: A Practical Introduction*. London: HMSO.

Becker, H. (1932). *Systematic Sociology on the Basis of the Beziehungslehre and Gebildelehre of Leopold von Wiese*. New York: Wiley.

Beckford, J. A. (1978). Through the Looking-Glass and out the Other Side: Withdrawal from Reverend Moon's Unification Church. *Archives de Sciences Sociales Des Religions* 23 (45.1): 95–116.

Berg, D. (1977). Love is News! *The Family of Love, MO Letters*, 8 February. www.xfamily.org/images/f/f0/Love-is-news-part1.pdf. Accessed 26 June 2023.

Berglie, P.-A. (1996). *Scientology: A Comparison with Religions of the East and West*. Los Angeles, CA: Freedom.

Borowik, C. (2023). *From Radical Jesus People to Virtual Religion: The Family International*. Cambridge: Cambridge University Press.

British Association for the Study of Religions (BASR). (2019). Ethical Guidelines. https://basrblog.files.wordpress.com/2019/09/basr-ethics-guidelines-final-17092019.pdf. Accessed 13 February 2023.

Brown, K. M. (1991). *Mama Lola: A Vodou Priestess in the Brooklyn*. Berkeley, CA: University of California Press.

Burt, A. R. (2023). *Hare Krishna in the Twenty-First Century*. Cambridge: Cambridge University Press.

Chryssides, G. D. (1991). *The Advent of Sun Myung Moon*. London: Macmillan.

Chryssides, G. D. (2010). How Prophecy Succeeds: Jehovah's Witnesses and Prophetic Expectations. *International Journal for the Study of New Religions* 1 (1), Spring: 27–48.

Chryssides, G. D. (ed.) (2011). *Heaven's Gate: Post-modernity and Popular Culture in a Suicide Group*. Farnham: Ashgate.

Chryssides, G. D. (2012). New Religious Movements: How Should New Religious Movements Be Defined? In M. Luck (ed.), *Philosophical Explorations of New and Alternative Religious Movements*. Farnham: Ashgate: 11–29.

Chryssides, G. D. (2016). *Jehovah's Witnesses: Continuity and Change*. London: Routledge.

Chryssides, G. D. (2017). The Welsh Connection: Pastor Joshua McCabe's Role in the Unification Church's Early History. *Acta Comparanda* Subsidia VI: 85–100.

Chryssides, G. D. (2022). *Jehovah's Witnesses: A New Introduction*. London: Bloomsbury.

Chryssides, G. D. and D. Cohn-Sherbok (2023). *The Covid Pandemic and the World's Religions*. London: Bloomsbury.

Chryssides, G. D. and R. A. Geaves (2014). *The Study of Religion: An Introduction to Key Ideas and Methods*. 2 ed. London: Bloomsbury.

Chryssides, G. D. and S. E. Gregg (eds.) (2019). *The Insider/Outsider Debate: New Perspectives in the Study of Religion*. Sheffield: Equinox.

Clarke, P. (ed.). (1987). *The New Evangelists*. London: Ethnographica.

Cowan, D. E. (2011). The Internet. In M. Stausberg and P. Edler (eds.), *The Routledge Handbook of Research Methods in the Study of Religion*. London: Routledge: 459–73.

Craig, W. (2022). The History of the Internet in a Nutshell. www.webfx.com/blog/web-design/the-history-of-the-internet-in-a-nutshell. Accessed 18 May 2023.

Cusack, C. (2010). *Invented Religions: Imagination, Fiction and Faith*. Farnham: Ashgate.

Daeson Jinrihoe (2023). Temple Stay. http://eng.daesoon.org/app/en/temples/stay. Accessed 16 May 2023.

Darley, J. M. and C. D. Batson (1973). From Jerusalem to Jericho: A Study of Situational and Dispositional Variables in Helping Behavior. *Journal of Personality and Social Psychology* 27: 100–08.

Davies, C. M. (1874). *Unorthodox London: or Phases of Religious Life in the Metropolis*. London: Tinsley Brothers.

Davies, H. (1954). *Christian Deviations*. London: SCM.

Dawson, A. (2010). Positionality and Role-Identity in a New Religious Context: Participant Observation at Céu do Mapià. *Religion* 40: 173–81.

Department of Health, Education, and Welfare (DHEW) (1978). *The Belmont Report: Ethical Principles and Guidelines for the Protection of Human Subjects of Research*. Bethesda: National Commission for the Protection of Human Subjects of Biomedical and Behavioural Research.

Dyck, M. and G. Allen (2013). Is Mandatory Research Ethics Reviewing Ethical? *Journal of Medical Ethics* 39: 517–20.

Ellwood, R. S. and H. B. Partin (1988). *Religious and Spiritual Groups in Modern America*. 2 ed. Englewood Cliffs, NJ: Prentice Hall.

Evans-Pritchard, E. E. (1951). *Social Anthropology*. London: Cohen and West.

Family Federation for World Peace and Unification (2017). A Man with a Mission – Part 3. https://familyfedihq.org/2017/06/a-man-with-a-mission-part-3. Accessed 17 May 2023.

Festinger, L., H. W. Riecken, and S. Schachter (1956). *When Prophecy Fails: A Social and Psychological Study of a Modern Group that Predicted the Destruction of the World*. Minneapolis: University of Minnesota Press.

Fine, G. A. (1993). Ten Lies of Ethnography: Moral Dilemmas in Field Research. *Journal of Contemporary Ethnography* 22: 267.

Folk, H. (2021). Jehovah's Witnesses and Sexual Abuse: 2. Belgium and The Netherlands, *Bitter Winter*, 13 January. https://bitterwinter.org/jehovahs-wit nesses-and-sexual-abuse-2-belgium-and-the-netherlands/. Accessed 1 March 2021.

Gregg, S. E. and L. Scholefield (2015). *Engaging with Living Religion: A Guide to Fieldwork in the Study of Religion*. London: Routledge.

Gregg, S. E. and G. D. Chryssides (2017). The Silent Majority? Understanding Apostate Testimony beyond 'Insider/Outsider' Binaries in the Study of New Religions. In E. V. Gallagher (ed.), *Visioning New and Minority Religions: Projecting the Future*. London: Routledge: 20–32.

Harvey, G. (2003a). Guesthood as Ethical Decolonising Research Method. *Numen: International Review for the History of Religions* 50 (2): 125–46.

Harvey, G. (2023b). Indigenous Religions. In G. D. Chryssides and A. R. Whitehead (eds.), *Contested Concepts in the Study of Religion: A Critical Exploration*. London: Bloomsbury: 57–62.

Haworth, I. (2001). *Cults: A practical guide*. London: Cult Information Centre (UK).

Heelas, P. (1988). Self-Religions in Britain. *Religion Today* 1 (1): 4–5.

Højsgaard, M. T. and M. Warburg (eds.) (2005). *Religion and Cyberspace*. London: Routledge.

Holden, A. (2002). *Jehovah's Witnesses: Portrait of a Contemporary Religious Movement*. London: Routledge.

Holy Spirit Association for the Unification of One of Christianity (1985). *The Tradition, Book One*. New York: Rose of Sharon Press.

Introvigne, M. (2022a). *Brainwashing*. Cambridge: Cambridge University Press.

Introvigne, M. (2022b). Jehovah's Witnesses and Sexual Abuse: The Court of Brussels Finds the CIAOSN Report Ill-Founded. *Bitter Winter*, 21 June. https://bitterwinter.org/jehovahs-witnesses-and-sexual-abuse/. Accessed 18 May 2023.

Jones, W. ([1784] 1876). *On the Gods of Greece, Italy and India*. Calcutta: Ghose.

Kawanishi, E. (2021). After Fieldwork: Vestiges in/from a Fieldworker. In C. Coker, G. Kajimaru and K. Kazama (eds.), *The Anthropology of Ba: Place and Performance Co-emerging*. Kyoto: Kyoto University Press: 158–76.

Kliever, L. D. (1994). *Scientology: A Worshipping Community [booklet]*. Los Angeles, CA: Freedom.

Kliever, L. D. (1995). *The Reliability of Apostate Testimony About New Religious Movements [booklet]*. Los Angeles, CA: Freedom.

Krüger, O. (2005). Discovering the Invisible Internet: Methodological Aspects of Researching Religion on the Internet. *Heidelberg Journal of religions on the Internet* 1(1): 1–27. https://heiup.uni-heidelberg.de/journals/index.php/religions/article/view/385. Accessed 26 June 2023.

Lewis J. R. (2019). Monolithic Inferences: Misinterpreting AUM Shinrikyo. *Journal of Religion and Violence* 7 (1): 44–54.

Ling, T. (1967). *History of Religions East and West*. London: Macmillan.

Lofland, J. (1966). *Doomsday Cult: A Study of Conversion, Proselytization, and Maintenance of Faith*. Englewood Cliffs, NJ: Prentice-Hall.

Martin, W. ([1965] 1985). *The Kingdom of the Cults*. Minneapolis, MN: Bethany House.

Melton, J. G. and R. L. Moore (1982). *The Cult Experience: Responding to the New Religious Pluralism*. New York: Pilgrim Press.

Mickler, M. L. (2022). *The Unification Church Movement*. Cambridge: Cambridge University Press.

Miller, L. (1997). Deaths Rouse New Attention on Web. *USA Today* (28 March).

Palmer, S. J. (1994). *Aliens Adored: Raël's UFO Religion*. New Brunswick, NJ: Rutgers University Press.

Palmer, S. J. (2004). Renegade Researchers, Radical Religions, Recalcitrant Ethics Boards: Towards the 'McDonaldization' of Social Research in North America. *Fieldwork in Religion* 12 (2): 239–58.

Palmer, S. J. (2017). Renegade Researchers, Radical Religions, Recalcitrant Ethics Boards: Towards the "McDonaldization" of Social Research in North America. *Fieldwork in Religion* 12.2: 239–58.

Popper, K. R. ([1963] 2002). *Conjectures and Refutations: The Growth of Scientific Knowledge*. London: Routledge.

Primiano, L. N. (1995). Vernacular Religion and the Search for Method in Religious Folklife. *Western Folklore* 54 (1): 37–56.

Ratnapāla, N. (1979). *The Beggar in Sri Lanka*. New Town Gothatuwa, Sri Lanka: Sarvodaya Vishva Lekha.

Redfield, R. (1956). *Peasant Society and Culture: An Anthropological Approach*. Chicago: University of Chicago Press.

Smart, N. (1979). *The Phenomenon of Christianity*. London: Collins.

Smart, N. (1995). *Worldviews: Crosscultural Explorations of Human Beliefs*. 2 ed. Englewood Cliffs, NJ: Prentice Hall.

Smith, G., S. Donaldson, and C. Roberts (1997). Cults Using the Web for Recruitment? *This Week* (30 March).

Smith, W. C. (1959). Comparative Religion: Whither – and Why? In M. Eliade and J. M. Kitagawa (eds.), *The History of Religions: Essays in Methodology*. Chicago: University of Chicago Press: 31–58.

Straits Times. (2016). Religious 'Relics' of Modern-Day Messiah Sun Myung Moon Go on Display in South Korea. *The Straits Times – Asia*, 18 February. www.straitstimes.com/asia/east-asia/religious-relics-of-modern-day-messiah-sun-myung-moon-go-on-display-in-south-korea. Accessed 5 June 2023.

Stroup, H. H. (1945). *The Jehovah's Witnesses*. New York: Columbia University Press.

Universities UK (2022). The Concordat to Support Research Integrity. www.universitiesuk.ac.uk/topics/research-and-innovation/concordat-support-research-integrity. Accessed 17 May 2023.

University of Georgia (n.d.). A Brief History of the Internet. www.usg.edu/galileo/skills/unit07/internet07_02.phtml. Accessed 18 May 2022.

Utrecht University (2020). Discontent among part of Jehovah's Witnesses about internal handling of abuse complaints. www.uu.nl/en/news/discontent-among-part-of-jehovahs-witnesses-about-internal-handling-of-abuse-complaints. Accessed 18 May 2023.

Vrijhof, P. H. and J. Waardenburg (eds.) (1977). *Official and Popular Religion: Analysis of a Theme for Religious Studies*. The Hague: Mouton.

Waddell, L. A. (1895). *The Buddhism of Tibet or Lamaism, With Its Mystic Cults, Symbolism and Mythology and in Its Relation to Indian Buddhism*. 1st ed. London: W. H. Allen.

Ward, W. (1817). *A View of the History, Literature, and Religion of the Hindoos* (Vol.1). London: Black, Parbury and Allen.

Watch Tower (2020). *'Shepherd the Flock of God'*. Wallkill: Christian Congregation of Jehovah's Witnesses.

Weber, J. (2018). Christian, What Do You Believe? Probably a Heresy about Jesus, Says Survey. *Christianity Today.* 16 October. www.christianitytoday.com/news/2018/october/what-do-christians-believe-ligonier-state-theology heresy.html. Accessed 20 December 2018.

Weber, M. ([1922] 1956). *The Sociology of Religion*. London: Methuen.

Westbrook, D. (2019). *Among the Scientologists*. New York: Oxford University Press.

Wilson, B. R. (1994). *Apostates and New Religious Movements [booklet]*. Los Angeles, CA: Freedom.

World Medical Organization (1996). Declaration of Helsinki. *British Medical Journal* 313 (7070) (December 7): 1448–49.

Yinger, J. M. (1946). *Religion in the Struggle for Power*. Durham: Duke University Press.

Acknowledgements

After several decades of fieldwork, there are many colleagues, students, and NRM members and ex-members to whom I am indebted. Many of these ideas have been discussed at conferences, particularly the British Association for the Study of Religions (BASR), the Center for Studies in New Religions (CESNUR) Studies, and INFORM (Information Network Focus on Religious Movements). Over the years many students have accompanied me on fieldwork, and discussed its implications both formally in seminars, and informally. Among colleagues, I am particularly grateful to Amy Whitehead and Stephen Jacobs for reading drafts of the manuscript and making extremely helpful comments. Thanks also to the late James R. Lewis, and to Rebecca Moore, who invited me to present these ideas in this volume, and has made many valuable suggestions while meticulously editing the manuscript. Last but not least, I would like to express my gratitude to my wife Margaret, who has endured many lengthy discussions on NRMs, and accompanied me on various field visits.

Cambridge Elements

New Religious Movements

Founding Editor

† James R. Lewis

Wuhan University

James R. Lewis was Professor of Philosophy at Wuhan University, China. He was the editor or co-editor of four book series, was the general editor for the *Alternative Spirituality and Religion Review*, and the associate editor for the *Journal of Religion and Violence*. His publications include *The Cambridge Companion to Religion and Terrorism* (Cambridge University Press 2017) and *Falun Gong: Spiritual Warfare and Martyrdom* (Cambridge University Press 2018).

Series Editor

Rebecca Moore

San Diego State University

Rebecca Moore is Emerita Professor of Religious Studies at San Diego State University. She has written and edited numerous books and articles on Peoples Temple and the Jonestown tragedy. Publications include *Beyond Brainwashing: Perspectives on Cultic Violence* (Cambridge University Press 2018) and *Peoples Temple and Jonestown in the Twenty-First Century* (Cambridge University Press 2022). She is reviews editor for *Nova Religio*, the quarterly journal on new and emergent religions published by the University of Pennsylvania Press.

About the Series

Elements in New Religious Movements go beyond cult stereotypes and popular prejudices to present new religions and their adherents in a scholarly and engaging manner. Case studies of individual groups, such as Transcendental Meditation and Scientology, provide in-depth consideration of some of the most well known, and controversial, groups. Thematic examinations of women, children, science, technology, and other topics focus on specific issues unique to these groups. Historical analyses locate new religions in specific religious, social, political, and cultural contexts. These examinations demonstrate why some groups exist in tension with the wider society and why others live peaceably in the mainstream. The series highlights the differences, as well as the similarities, within this great variety of religious expressions. To discuss contributing to this series please contact Professor Moore.

Cambridge Elements ☰

New Religious Movements

Elements in the Series

Printed in the United States
by Baker & Taylor Publisher Services